CW00503856

OUT ON A LIMBANG

Alan Shoubridge

Out on a Limbang
Alan Shoubridge

All rights reserved. No part of this publication may be reproduced, stored in any retrieval system or transmitted in any form or by any means, electronic, mechanical, photocopying, recording or otherwise, without the prior written permission of the copyright holder for which application should be addressed in the first instance to the publishers. The views expressed herein are those of the author and do not necessarily reflect the opinion or policy of Tricorn Books or the employing organisation, unless specifically stated. No liability shall be attached to the author, the copyright holder or the publishers for loss or damage of any nature suffered as a result of the reliance on the reproduction of any of the contents of this publication or any errors or omissions in the contents.

ISBN 9781912821778
A CIP catalogue record for this
book is available from the British Library.
Published 2020

Tricorn Books
Aspex Gallery, 42 The Vulcan Building
Gunwharf Quays
Portsmouth PO1 3BF

Printed & bound in the UK

OUT ON A LIMBANG

contents

Foreword

This Story is Based on Fact

At dawn on 12thDecember 1962, 55 elite Royal Marine Commandos and 4 Royal Navy personnel carried out a dawn attack on the town of Limbang, Sarawak, Borneo to rescue hostages taken by Indonesian rebels. They included the Governor, his wife, the Chief of Police and 11 others. They were due to be executed that morning.

The marines were told to expect resistance from between 100-150 well armed rebels. Statistics later showed there were between 400-600 highly armed rebels waiting for them.

The hostages were successfully rescued but at a cost of 5 Royal Marines lives and 15 badly injured.

This story relates especially to the Vickers Medium Machine Gun Section (MMGs) of Support Company. After the initial landing, the MMGs were often sent out on their own to complete various tasks away from the remainder of the Company. This suited them well.

The language and the rhetoric is typical of what one would expect from all Service personnel, especially in combat situations at the time. Humour plays an important part in such circumstances, relieving stress and anxiety at difficult times.

Some of the "activities" are just part of the story and all names have been changed.

The war in Borneo lasted a further 3 years. Little was known in UK about this war as media focus was constantly on the war in Vietnam.

This book is a tribute to those who lost their lives, the injured and the professionalism of the Royal Marine Corps.

Singapore

Singapore 1962. Darkness had fallen over the Naval Air Station, the silence broken only by the constant chatter of the countless insects that inhabited the grass and monsoon ditches around the base

Occasionally, music from a transistor radio somewhere up in the accommodation blocks filtered through to the wandering sentries as they patrolled the four square mile complex, a welcome change from the continual hum of the nagging mosquitoes and croaking toads. One area however was a complete contrast. The NAAFI. Situated above the dining hall and galley the Other Ranks Recreation Area throbbed to the beat of the noisy juke-box that greedily consumed the constant wave of ten cent coins it was fed. A bawdy, shouting, swearing holocaust where the Tiger beer flowed as though there were no tomorrows. For some there was not.

The Commando unit's first night back in base after an operation was always the same. While the "married fads" got home to their families in the huge Sembawang Hills Estate, the remainder congregated in the canteen drinking as much of the cheap beer as they could consume whilst trying to remain sober enough to stagger ashore when the bar closed. After a months' compulsory abstinence and the ensuing tiredness of the long trek back from the patrols on the Thailand border, many had not the tenacity to survive the pace and drunkenly crawled back to their billets and oblivion.

Not unusually, a fight developed at one end of the bar between a wiry, fervently patriotic Welshman and a big ex-miner from Newcastle; nobody except those in the immediate vicinity whose liquor was being jeopardised showed the slightest interest even as the Welshman crashed into the juke-box where he decided to sleep awhile. Unperturbed, interested only in their own burbled conversations, all were unaware of the arrival of the Duty Sergeant Major at the head of the stairs.

Though not for long.

Seated in the far corner at a table conveniently near the bar yet just away from the mass, Scouse Lee and Al Lewis immediately spotted the new arrival across the crowded assembly.

Lee and Lewis were two machine-gunners from Support Company. Whichever of the five Commando units within the Royal Marines they were drafted to, either in UK or abroad, Machine-gunners, Mortar men, Anti-tank ranks and Assault engineers, the four platoons that comprised Support Company, they could be assured that a buddy from a previous commission would be in Support Company of their new unit, so, not unnaturally, a bond grew over the years between the ranks of this Company; an *espirit de corps* that the rifle companies did not experience,

This was an especially good period of time for the young marines, both aged twenty-one, as their eighteen month tour of duty with 42 Commando RM was almost at an end and in just two months they were to be repatriated to the United Kingdom. No more mosquitoes or leeches or bloody camel spiders. Just Blighty, real beer and good women.

Whilst they couldn't wait to get back to England, they sat and reflected on the good times they'd had on their first commission abroad; Hong Kong(twice), East Africa, Australia, Aden, Borneo, Bahrain, Malaya and many more obscure places they had visited and sampled the local delights. And Singapore itself. From the fantastically sculptured Tiger Balm Gardens where Chinese characters came almost to life, to the brightly lit streets densely populated with every nationality conceivable bustling about in a continual mass of colour; the tri-shaws and rick-shaws; the stalls laden with all manner of foods and souvenirs; the bars which spilled out into the streets, the pimps and prostitutes that accosted one on every street corner. A fascinating place in its own right and one which, as members of the all conquering unit soccer team they had been fortunate enough to explore at greater lengths than many in the unit. For on several occasions they had remained back in Sembawang while the unit took part in exercises up in Malaya, to play in important league and cup matches. The unit team had remained undefeated all season and both had collected an array of cups and medals. Lewis had gained not inconsiderable fame for his goal scoring feats (67 in 20 games) and often in newspapers delivered to the unit up country, morale would be boosted by reports of his and the unit's achievements. Lee, a football fanatic in the true Liverpool tradition and a good player, never ceased to amaze his comrades by combining his insatiable thirst for the local brew with fantastic fitness. Though similar in height to Lewis, Lee was far the stockier of the two and the stronger having also represented the unit at both boxing and weightlifting.

As an Elvis Presley record appropriately finished just as Duty Sergeant Major Lawrence reached the machine and pulled out the plug, the jeers and catcalls of the inebriated ranks died as he turned to face the throng with a typically icy stare at once commanding the respect and virtual silence he demanded.

"What the bloody hell does he want?" murmured Lee in a voice he instantly realised was too loud, as Lawrence glared at him from the opposite end of the room, resplendent in his immaculately starched khaki uniform and spotless white belt and gaiters.

"What I want, Marine Lee is for you and the other ranks of Support Company and those of L Company to get your arses back to your billets and commence packing your gear ready to move out tonight. The remainder of you can stop sniggering because all shore leave is stopped as from now and the bar is closed forthwith. Do I make myself quite clear?" asked the crinkly haired, tall and unpopular Lawrence known amongst the ranks as Lollipop, who, on beckoning the barman behind the bar to close it at once, turned on his heels and strode out of the room.

"Shave off. Where the hell are we off to now? What's the betting our bloody repat will be fucked up?" moaned Lewis.

"Nah. It's probably some more riots up at KL" said Lee referring to a previous stint they'd been called upon to sort out in Kuala Lumpar a few months earlier.

"Yeah" brightened Lewis. "And we'll obviously be rear-party as we're due home shortly"

"Let's go and see what the buzz is then."

Consuming the remainder of their ale in one swallow they filtered through the throng and down the stairs into the relatively cool night air.

"We should've gone ashore earlier; bin safe in some brothel by now."

"Bloody shore-patrol will be all over Singers now dragging the bastards out."

"Yeah, but the buzz will have got round by now, so the clever sods will have got themselves nicely tucked up for the night somewhere."

"Don't suppose we could do a "Houdini"?" proffered Lewis

"No need. They won't take us two. Too near repat."

"Where have I heard that before? C'mon."

On reaching the accommodation block Lewis was immediately re-directed to the armoury for weapon and ammunition supply duties, while Lee continued up the two flights of stairs to Support Company's billets, at the top of the block. The atmosphere he found on entering their room was distinctly unfavourable for already two of the "married fads" had been brought back to camp and were not pleased.

The eight-man sparsely furnished room, in which each man had one bed and one locker only, comprised four Assault engineers, two Mortar men and Lee and Lewis from Machine-guns. In overall charge of the room was Corporal Reed, an engineer of no mean ability though who came in for substantial ribbing from the other members of the Company for his almost paranoiac love of himself. Tall , fair and heavily built with continually peeling skin on his nose Reed was at this moment in a quandary, as usual, panicking about the three men missing from his room. Seeing Lee, the relief was plainly visible until he realised Lewis was not with him. "Where the bloody hell's Lewis, Lee?"

"Don't panic, he's issuing bullets for you buggers down the armoury."

"And for you too. We're all off on this jaunt together," replied Reed.

"But we're due for repat......." Started Lee.

"Tough."

"Anyone know the whereabouts of Tug Wilson?" asked Reed , and on receiving a negative reply "in some brothel by now I assume."

"If he's got any sense. Where the rest of us should be, too, if we had any bloody sense" said Morris, a thin Mortarman with a head that physically appeared far too large for the rest of his body to carry.

The shore-patrol will pick him up," started Reed

"Wanna bet?" volunteered Lee.

"OK. that's enough for now. Just pin back yer luggoles and listen to what I have to say. Now, there's apparently some trouble in Borneo; some revolutionaries have decide to try and take it over or something, things aren't too clear at the moment - and because we are so bloody wonderful, though you wouldn't think so to look at the state of you lot at the moment, the powers that be have decided to send us over there to sort the buggers out. In one hour from now we will parade outside fully booted and spurred in the same rig we use for the "up country" jaunts plus ammunition you will now draw from the armoury where friend Lewis supposedly is. Or better be" said Reed glaring at Lee. " So get your gear packed, if you've bothered to unpack yet, and get down to the Company Store to load stores. And that includes you Price if you don't mind?" Reed added sarcastically to the huge, balding Scotsman spread out on his bed inflating a Durex as if it were a balloon.

"I won't be needing this bugger then, will I?" he replied releasing the air from it and allowing it to whizz round the room to the amusement of all.

"What about our repat though?" persisted Lee

"You go unless anyone says anything different" said Reed

"Bloody Indos. Why couldn't they wait a few weeks before having a punch up?"

"Yeah, but just think Scouse, we'll see some action and you'll probably get a VC." said Morris

"Bloody VD's more like it. Lewis'll bust a gut when he finds we're included in this lot."

As the Companies loaded their stores and ammunition, into the three-tonners, the mood amongst them varied between false bravado on the part of the younger members to utter dismay from the married fads to whom no-one was inclined to say too much - not while they carried live ammunition.

Lee and Lewis also were not overjoyed at the situation but found some consolation in the fact that no-one appeared particularly bothered about the non-appearance of Tug Wilson who had only one month to go before repatriation so they figured that there was still hope for them to be left behind or, at the very worst, if they had to go it would be for a week or two at the most. For their replacements would surely be in Singapore soon and it would only take a month to acclimatise them.

Thirty minutes later they were aboard the trucks and heading out of the base,

"They won't take us, the bastard said... so what the fuck am I doing on the back of this bleedin wagon? Heading for Singapore National Airport? No, heading for bastard Changi RAF base and a bloody great Beverly that's going to fly me into the bloody Ulu again for a few more meals for fucking mossies and leeches" drawled Lee. Lewis opposite him at the back of the lorry laughed with the rest of the marines at Lee's predicament, adding "Yeah, but not for long. We'll soon be back down here again" he said referring to the notorious Nee Soon village they had just entered. A favourite amongst the marines due to its closeness to their base, Nee Soon was a sprawling area of market stalls, bars, brothels, tattoo artists, open cafés, and souvenir shops. It was the common practice for the marines to stagger down to Nee Soon after the NAFFI closed and therefore the cheap booze, failed to be available, for Nee Soon never closed. Tonight as usual, the village was a conglomeration of rickshaws, cars and pedestrians all attempting to claim a part of the narrow roadway as they shuffled along. Nothing and no-one hurried in Nee Soon.

As the lorries slowly edged their way through, every now and then above the blare of the music, claxons and hubble, a cheer would ascend from groups of marines on the sidewalks as they recognised the markings on the trucks rolling past whilst keeping an eye out for the prowling shore-patrols that were trying to round up those on shore-leave to herd them back to base. A short distance further along the street they reached the famously notorious Spotlight Bar; not the largest in the village, but by far the most popular with its reputation for having the most beautiful barmaids and hostesses and the best food. Coloured lights played around the entrance to the Wild West styled bar whilst inside East met West in the most affable circumstances. It was as they were passing the bar that Lee and Lewis, the two "tail end charlies" at the back of the truck picked out a familiar face amongst the throng around the bar. Tug Wilson.

Wilson, all six feet four of him, had got the buzz alright that the unit was on the move, but no bugger was going to get him back in the bloody jungle. Not with a month to do!

"Tug...hey Tug!" yelled Lee trying to attract his attention above the collusion of noise.

Wilson was just entering the bar, or perhaps staggering into it would have been a better description for, without the support of the beautiful Chinese girl around whose shoulders he was draped, he must surely have fallen. However, the sound of the familiar voice did somehow penetrate his brain, as, in one easy movement his hand left the shapely buttock of the girl and majestically rose in a long, slow two-finger gesture towards the now cheering troops. Reid, up front with the driver would be none the wiser being unable to distinguish one lot of cheering from all that was going on in the village about him.

Laboriously through the heavy traffic, the wagons rolled towards Changi until at last they reached the Air Force base.

"Everybody out. Unload the stores, then get fell in, in three ranks without a load of cackle and on the double. Move!" Short squat and almost bald, "Punchy" Nelson was not a Sergeant-Major to be argued with at the best of times, and now, as a married fad himself, was not one of the times. An ex Amateur Boxing Association champion, he reigned supreme in the Senior NCO's Mess especially when full of Tiger when his party-piece was to explain and demonstrate on anyone he had a particular dislike of, exactly how he won his title. By a knockout.

To Borneo

In remarkably short time, the huge Beverly aircraft lumbered along the runway and , fully laden with marines and stores lifted its bulging mass into the black skies, rapidly leaving behind the lights of Singapore and Malaya as it winged across the Indian Ocean towards Brunei, British North Borneo.

Half an hour later as the plane shuddered throughout the night, the skipper's voice crackled across the intercom "We are running into some heavy weather. Fasten all seat belts and extinguish cigarettes."

"That's all we bloody need" said Lewis. I've got a head like Spithead as it is."

Soon, through the portholes, they could see bright flashes of lightning illuminating the banks of cloud about them, while even over the drone of the engines they could hear the peels of thunder outside. Suddenly the aircraft banked steeply, then dropped dramatically as it was tossed around by the raging storm through which they had no choice but to pass. Several of the marines were now slumped forward in their seats, their faces thrust into the paper bags provided for such occasions.

Flying an old aircraft in a tropical storm was no joy ride at the best of times, and after the night's intake of Tiger it was decidedly worse for the marines. For an hour the Beverly battled through the storm until the skipper informed them that they were starting their descent, at the same time warning that conditions were no different at ground level in Brunei and that they could expect a bumpy landing.

Apprehensive, and with some still feeling decidedly unwell, the marines braced themselves for the landing; streaks of light were now plainly visible though these rapidly vanished as they descended into the black abyss of cloud between them and the runway. Then suddenly, the inside of the plane was plunged into darkness, immediately explained by the pilot as an electrical fault which, he hoped would not interfere with their capability to land.

"I hope this RAF bastard knows what he's on" said Lee

"Not much we can fuckin' do about it if he don't, is there?" replied Lewis .

Twice the aircraft circled the sparse ill-lit airfield, the anxious pilot straining his eyes through the torrent of water on the windscreen for the best approach. His decision made, the plane dropped, levelled out and came in to land. Hearts in mouths, the marines tensed themselves for the touchdown, the engines roaring as they strained to slow the craft down. Finally the wheels made contact with the runway as the plane bumped along the uneven ground,.

"Thank Christ for that" somebody put everyone's thoughts into words. But no sooner had he spoken than they were thrust back into their seats as the engines roared again and the plane lurched forward and took off, rising sharply and steeply.

"The bloody idiot's overshot. stupid RAF bastard."

"Can't be easy. At least we're still in one piece."

"For how much fucking' longer?"

Once again the aircraft circled and came into land. This time the skill of the much maligned pilot was adequate and the plane shuddered to a halt, skidding the last few feet and coming to rest at the very edge of the runway.

"Fuck my old sea boots. Get that bleedin' door open and let's get out of this thing before he fucks off again." said lee.

As they unstrapped themselves from their seats Lieutenant Robson, the Company Commander, moved to the front of the aircraft.

"Pay-attention-all-off-you" stuttered Robson, a slim, tall man with a thick moustache who hailed from Rhodesia. Well liked by the rank and file, Robson was unfortunate enough to be born with a speech impediment and his deep, jerky voice was often mimicked by the troops. But he was popular with them because he was approachable and fair.

"The-Sarawak-Rangers-are-defending-the-airfield-apparently,-we-will-disembark-and-make-forthe-main-terminal-building-at-the-edge-of-the-runway.This-airfield-has-been-under-attack-today-but-you-will-disembark-from-the-rear."

"I dunno what's worse, a ride on this fucking thing or getting fired at." debated Price, looking very pale.

As the hatch doors opened the full impact of the storm thrust itself upon them. Quickly filing out off the aircraft they headed for the transit building barely visible through the torrential rain, but no sooner had Lee and Lewis covered twenty yards than they came under fire. Single shots ricocheted off the tarmac around them, stinging them into a frantic race for cover, which at last they found, diving under the dark mass that appeared before them at the edge of the airport. While it was not the building they had been instructed to make for it was certainly a port in the storm and as they lay there they could hear still the sound of fire from the far side of the runway.

"Bloody hell, I'm knackered" panted Lee,

"Where's the firing coming from?"

"Christ knows. I just hope those bloody Rangers know we're on their side."

After a few moments silence ,the piercing voice of Punchy Nelson yelled at all around to stay where they were until further orders.

"Where the fuck does he think we're going to go from here?" said Lewis, the sweat and rain pouring from his face as his eyes strained to see through the darkness which slowly was beginning to clear enough for them to vaguely make out the silhouettes of surrounding objects.

For twenty minutes they lay there, hearts pounding, ever alert waiting for something to happen as the dawn slowly crept in and mercifully the rain eased. Turning, they could see the Beverly out on the runway, a shiny, sliver, ghost-like shape, barely six feet from the end of the tarmac at the very edge of the jungle. Looking more closely at their immediate surround Lee's heart suddenly gave a lurch. They realised that they were under a vehicle of some description but in their haste to find protection they cared little. Now, however, it became crystal clear to Lee that they had taken refuge under a very large tanker.

"Hey, Lewy, d'you know what we're under?"

"Some sort of waggon, eh?"

"Yeah. What sort of waggons are around airports though?"

"Shit" as the realisation dawned on Lewis.

"Time to rev up and fuck off I reckon."

"One bullet in this thing and ....." said Lewis looking up at the huge tanker used for storing the highly explosive Avgas that refuels aircraft.

"Everybody into the Transit building" yelled Nelson, now boldly strolling around the building itself, posting sentries at each corner. Inside, the sparsely furnished waiting room consisting of a long reception counter and two circular cushion seats situated in the centre of the room, was now a mass of sprawling bodies as the marines settled wherever there was space. Occasionally one would enter the toilet and the sounds of retching could plainly be heard, whether from the effect of the Tiger, the flight, or fear, or a combination of all three none could be sure. Some of the marines broke into the twenty-four hour ration packs they had been issued with in Singapore, though all sparingly as there was no knowing where the next supply of food would come from. Steam rose from their saturated combat suits as the temperature within the room increased; wet cigarettes were finally lit; the room became a damp, sweaty, smokey, steaming area alleviated only by the two open windows at the opposite end to the entrance. Robson was trying to explain the situation around the airport and Brunei town itself. At that moment the door to the hall opened and two Sarawak Rangers entered the room, the latter at the head of a stretcher he and a third Ranger were carrying. An audible silence fell in the room for on the stretcher, wrapped in parachute silk was a body, blood seeping through the silk and congealing halfway along its length. Stunned into silence, the marines watched as the Rangers placed the stretcher in one corner of the room and stood silent guard over it.

"So it's not an exercise after all" said Morris trying to stop shaking.

19

Brunei

Robson then called an 'O' Group for the Platoon Commanders and Nelson, Fisher from Mortars, Rice from Assault Engineers and 'Baron' Knight from Machine Guns attended whilst the remainder of the marines warily eyed the body of the Ranger as they awaited the outcome.

"Shan't be sorry to get out of this place. Bloody heaves, what with sweaty bodies, dead bodies, smoke and steam, and a pan full of spew in the piss-house" said Luther a tall, ginger headed, fresh faced machine gunner.

"At least we're not getting shot at in here" said Lee.

"Wonder where we'll go from here and what sort of action we'll see when we do go" Baker thought aloud, his jet black hair plastered over his pitted face.

"I reckon we're just about to find out. Here comes Baron."

Baron Knight crossed the room to his platoon and ordered them into a corner where he proceeded to enlighten them on the situation. Six feet or thereabouts, Knight was immensely popular with his platoon. A large, overweight Sergeant with a huge beaming face, he had acquired the nickname 'Baron' through his apparently uncanny knack over the course of his sixteen years in the Corps of making substantial cash rewards from the sale of anything he could get his hands on. Always in trouble with his superiors, his tremendous sense of humour carried himself and his comrades through many a tough time, together with his love for Rudyard Kipling and Contract Bridge, either of which could consume all the spare time he could find. In his late thirties and married with seven children, Baron was as happy as he'd ever been in Singapore and, with his foreign service allowances and his 'transactions' was making a fortune.

"So it all boils down, my 'ansomes' that we don't know bugger all about what's happening. But we're going to move out to the Brunei Hotel in the centre of town and meet up with some of the local wallers and police and militia who'll put us in the picture and determine our next move, OK?"

"What about our repat?"

"Pick me up when I stop laughing" chuckled Baron to Lee's query.

A few minutes later they filed out of the building, warily searching for any movement that would give an enemy position away and proceeded down a long road leading from the airport into the town itself. Verging on the size of a small city, quite modern in the architecture of its buildings, Brunei was normally a busy, thriving place where, as an oil rich state in British Protectorate much business was transacted both local and international. As a result, even more modern buildings were under construction and to accommodate the businessmen that flew into Brunei the brand new Brunei Hotel was recently constructed. Reaching it, through the debris of buildings peppered with bullet holes, shattered glass strewn everywhere, litter, empty rifle magazines and bandoliers thrown away at random and mortar and brickwork spattered from the result of rocket fire hitting buildings, the marines slid into the hotel and gratefully, after sentries had again been posted, sank down wherever they could in the Reception Lounge. The wealth created by the oil industry of Brunei initiated an attempt at introducing to that state the grandeur to be found in other such societies and to this end, the Brunei Hotel had been built with Victorian splendour as its mentor. The bright, yet gaudy ceiling artwork was offset by the austere pillars and drab wallpapers while the dark wooden furniture gave the place a somewhat depressing and oppressive atmosphere. Furniture was smashed, statues broken, curtains ripped down and the wall showed evidence of an attack by both bullets and rockets, while the blood stains on the expensive carpeting showed evidence of substantial injuries sustained by some unfortunate.

"Just like our front room on a Friday night when the old man comes home pissed." said Lee, adding a moment of relaxed humour.

"Not exactly ready for COs rounds, is it?" murmured Laker, staring directly at the bloodstains.

"Wonder if we'll get a chance to look around. There must be a bar and galley here somewhere that we can explore'" said Baker.

"No chance of that my 'ansomes" called Baron as he rumbled across the room towards them. "I'm just off to an O Group so behave yourselves for five minutes. Keep an eye on these buggers Jock and don't let them wander away. We could be on the move at any time."

"Aye, Sarge" replied the tall, lean Scotsman who was the MMG Platoon Corporal. Standing six feet two inches tall with black curly hair cut in the traditional 'short back and sides', Jock Mackay was not a man to fool with, being a black belt in karate and extremely short tempered, especially when the supply of whisky was limited.

"Find out about our repat," called Lewis after the disappearing Baron.

Glancing over his shoulder, the plump Sergeant just laughed and continued over to a corner of the reception area that Robson had cordoned off for his meeting.

"Two weeks ago I was in a pub in Bradford telling some bloke I was off to sunny Singapore and a trip round the Far East for eighteen months. He kept telling me what a lucky bastard I was. Now look where the fuck I am!" said Gerald Theodor Moran in the broad Yorkshire drawl of his native County. Short and stocky, Moran, like his compatriot from Yorkshire, 'Geordie' Metcalf was fiercely proud of their lineage and defied anyone to ridicule their beloved county, especially on the subject of cricket about which both were fanatical. Metcalf, in contrast, was of medium height, medium appearance and medium intelligence. Both were married but had left their wives and four children (two apiece) in Yorkshire.

"Christ, that was quick," Macaky said to Baron as he headed for them and the O Group broke up.

"Wasn't long, was I? Did you miss me?" he smiled

"Of course. What's the buzz then?" asked Lewis.

Lowering his large frame onto the floor in front of his platoon. Baron said "Not a lot to tell really, my ansomes. No-one seems to know bugger all. Apparently the immediate area has been cleared of rebels for now, but we must remain vigilant - that's a good word, innit"? he smiled. "There'll be another O Group soon and we should know a bit more about what's going on then, so for now just lie low and relax."

The next O Group was called shortly afterwards and returning from it, Baron once again gathered his platoon about him. "Righto my sons, peg back yer lugs. this is the latest from Robbo - I mean Lieutenant Robson" - Baron corrected himself realising the close proximity of the Officer. "We're off on a little trip on a couple of 100 ton Ramp Cargo Lighters to a place called Limbang which is the Headquarters of the fifth Division of this state. it's about 12 miles south of here on the river Sungei Limbang and the geezer in charge of the place, a bloke called Harris, and a few other Europeans, about eight we think, are apparently being held captive by two hundred odd rebels in the cop shop there. Harris's missus and a couple of female secretaries are amongst this group, too, so the sooner we get them out the better, before they get man - handled by these rebels if they haven't already."

"Probably all up the stick by now" said Lee.

"They bloody soon will be if you get near them" said Lewis.

"OK, that's enough" ordered Baron. "As far as we know" he continued, "they are armed with mostly old musket-type flint lock rifles and a few Light Machine Guns. Limbang itself is roughly 700 yards long 100 yards wide, surrounded on three sides by jungle and the river on the other side. These rebels are supposed to be the hard core of the TNKU which, for your valued information stands for Tentara Nasional Kalimantan Utara, or, the North Kalimantan National Army. They're wearing arm bands and caps with this crap written all over it, so anything dressed in this rig can be eliminated, OK? Good. Now we've got a few hours rest before we move off around ten tonight, so get the guns checked over right away and ready for action 'cos they'll be taken down to the boats in an hour from now and loaded on board for us by the Rangers. Any questions?" Baron finished.

"Yeah. When do we eat, Sarge?"

"When the good Lord provides or when that fat sod in the galley gets off his arse" laughed their leader. "By the by, stay in this area lads so's I know where to find you if things change, OK?" he said over his shoulder as he left them.

"Sounds bloody dodgy to me" said Metcalf. "What the fuck are sixty of us going to do to two hundred well dug-in rebels?"

"Crap ourselves I expect" said Moran.

"Anyways, I'm getting my 'ead down while we can" said Baker

who, it was rumoured was capable of sleeping on a clothes line, or any place including whilst standing to attention on sentry duty. "Shake me halfway down - if I smile keep going, if I don't piss off"

"Wakey wakey. Rise and Shine. Hands off cocks on socks. Don't roll over, roll out. Come on my ansomes. ABC. All Bin Changed. Ten minutes to get fully booted and spurred."

"Where are we?" drawled a half asleep Lee.

"Bloody Butlins, where do you think?"

"Oh yeah, we're at war ain't we. I'm breaking my bloody neck. Going for a piss."

"Everybody ready?" hoped Robson

"All except Lee, sir. He's having a slash, er, I mean a piss. Sorry sir" bumbled Lewis.

"Alright. I suppose we'd better wait for him, though I'd rather not" spluttered Robson waiting for the spontaneous ripple of laughter that did not materialise. "Right then. If you are finally ready marine Lee, we will continue. Form up in single file and load your weapons as you reach the door. Keep your safety catches on at all times, unless of course we come under fire. There will be absolutely no talking from now until we reach the landing craft. Is that clearly understood?" Satisfied that everyone did understand, Robson led the way from the hotel into the dark night as they cautiously filed out from their refuge.

The shadows cast by the tall buildings in the semi full moonlight provided sufficient cover for the troops but they realised all too well that the same applied to a waiting enemy. Slowly, silently they headed for their rendezvous with the craft they were to board, moving quickly where bright patches of moonlight between the buildings marred their path. Suddenly, the still of the night was shattered by the loud, echoing report of a single shot, scattering the marines into a frenzied search for protection.

"Baker, you stupid bastard. You could've killed me" yelled Mackay shaking with fear and fury.

"Sorry, Jock. I couldn't help it. It just went off. Are you alright?"

"Course I'm bloody alright. Not thanks to you though. Pass the word on to Robbo that everything's OK. Accidental discharge" he ordered Linden, ahead of him.

"So much for silence." said Lewis. Might as well get the bloody Massed Bands along now."

"Shut up. And get moving."

Forty three minutes later, unscathed, they reached the boats that were to take them to Limbang. Now, the code of silence broken with the banter of the Sarawak Rangers as they loaded the craft with supplies and ammunition, the marines rested as Baron, Robson and two Naval Officers who had appeared from they knew not where, discussed the strategy for the landing, with the Company Commander of L Company and his subordinates. Their decisions reached, L Company and the MMG Platoon were divided equally and allotted a craft each, the machine guns being mounted just ahead of the bridge on the port side in both cases. Corporal Mackay, with Moran, Luther and Baker were designated the leading craft with Baron, Lee Lewis and Metcalf on the other. Now, they were ready to move off.

To Limbang

At midnight the two boats slowly nosed their way to the entrance of the harbour, the dull thudding of the engines echoing through the dark night, as their bows cut though the fluorescent water. The river Limbang was tidal, with many twists and turns and mud banks as it wound its way through the mangrove swamps. The two craft reached the start of the Limbang at 0200 and carefully negotiated the sharp bend into it from the main river from Brunei. The moon drifted behind a bank of cloud but now, because of the closeness of the banks on either side of the narrow river, the skippers were able to keep their crafts exactly in midstream, their only hazard being the continuous fallen trees and debris that constantly banged into the boats on the fast flowing river. For this was the rainy season in Borneo and the torrential rains and storms swept much of the surrounding jungle into the rivers and streams.

For another hour they slowly progressed, keeping a sharp lookout through the darkness that surrounded them for any unusual movements but, save for the occasional startled bird which scurried aloft with a piercing shriek, there were none. Now they had come to a slightly wider part of the river and here both boats simultaneously cut their engines and drifted along with the current, the only sound that of the water lapping gently against the sides of each craft as it edged forward. The word was passed that they had reached this point of their journey ahead of schedule and would idle here for half an hour. The Naval Officer commanding the leading boat radioed to his compatriot in the second that while a constant state of readiness must prevail, the troops were at liberty to talk and enjoy a last smoke before they pushed on, and the glow of lighted cigarettes and matches showed the strain on the faces of the tense marines.

"Got any nutty left Scouse?"

"Nah. Just pussers hard tack and bloody condensed milk. That'll have to do though."

"Anyone fancy a few prawns and crab to go with it?" said Baron

"Who said there was fuck all in the Brunei hotel?" he grinned, his large jovial face wreathed in smiles. "Have I ever let you down lads? I 'ad a bloody good scout round that hotel. That's why I was late for the O Group and knew next to bugger all about this little trip. By the time I got to the O Group it was bloody near over. Never mind, eh?"

"Organisation - the best thing in the Corps, eh Sarge?" said Lee.

"True my son, so true."

"I don't give a toss what happens now I've got some good grub in ma belly" said Kirk, one of the rifle company in a deep Yorkshire accent. An hour later he was dead.

"Yorkshire born Yorkshire bred. Thick in arm and thick in head."

"Bollicks."

"OK cut it out you two. Save it for the rebels." ordered Baron.

"Aye, careful what you say about the Master race, Lewy" said Baron.

"Naturally I didn't mean you Jack"

"Naturally."

"Right gentlemen. We're off. Best of luck to everyone" called the skipper, as the engines burst into life and the boats moved forward their speed increasing until they were almost full ahead.

"I think I want a crap" said someone.

"Hard shit" came the reply.

Just over half an hour later they could see the lights of Limbang forming a glow in the sky above the jungle to their front. Thin streaks of light started to appear in the black sky as dawn attempted to break through the black abyss of night. On they surged through the black water, that now grew lighter each minute as the dawn broke so quickly until, through the haze, they could see the wide right hand sweep of a bend in the river and the beginning of a town they instinctively knew must be Limbang.

"Get ready lads" yelled Baron. "Shoot first, questions later."

Suddenly all the lights in Limbang were extinguished, but it mattered little as the light was now more than adequate. Beads of sweat ran down foreheads into straining eyes; fingers on triggers were sticky and clammy; bodies strained to get as comfortable as possible in their firing positions.

"There she is lads" yelled Baron. "Stand by to repel boarders"

"Where does he think he is, fucking Trafalgar?"

For a town in the middle of nowhere, Limbang was unexpectedly modern; but mingled with the concrete buildings were wooden shacks especially at each end of the town. No building was more than one storey high and there appeared to be just one main street with four side roads off it running at ninety degrees from the river into the jungle. On the other bank was a small collection of shacks which appeared to be uninhabited because of their bad state of repair. No sooner had they reached the first bashers than the first hail of bullets rained on the craft from all along the river bank.

"Fire at will, Lads" came the order, which was totally unnecessary as the marines had already returned a devastating barrage to their enemy. The rat-tat-tat of the machine guns sent their deadly message ashore cutting down anything that was foolhardy enough to move.

Bullets sprayed the water about them and thudded into the sides of the boats splintering their wooden sides, ricocheting off and whining into the air, as they headed for the jetty two hundred yards ahead that was to be the landing stage for the rifle troops. Now the engines slowed making them an easier target and suddenly they saw a line of bullets raking across the water towards them from an automatic weapon ashore. Those in direct line shouted warnings and pressed hard against others to avoid the bullets, but what must have been the last round in the enemy's magazine, for then it stopped firing, caught the skipper in the knee and with a yell of pain he was down, blood spurting everywhere. Someone grabbed the wheel as a medic hauled him to the cover of the starboard side. Just then a figure ashore ran for cover behind a petrol pump situated on the bank of the river. As if by remote control, the machine guns on both boats trained on the pump and blew it and the body behind it to smithereens.

"Got the bastard" yelled Lewis. Give me another belt Jack, Jack for Chrisssake give me another belt" he shouted.

"ere" said Lee handing a fresh belt to Lewis. "Jack's shit it."

"Fucking hell. You bastards. Don't worry Jack, we'll wipe the fuckin' lot out now."

Another burst from the automatic ashore splashed harmlessly into the water near the boat but this time the firer was spotted and two machine guns and half a dozen rifles silenced it for good. Two fell almost at once, shot from close range by an enemy who was riddled with bullets before he had time to reflect on his efforts. Now the enemy were on the run, hotly pursued by the fighting marines who flushed out the more stubborn pockets of resistance with grenades and 3.5 rocket launchers. Another marine fell but still they surged on until they reached the police headquarters where the Americans and Europeans were captive. After a fierce and bloody onslaught the enemy fled and miraculously the unscathed hostages released. Meanwhile the second boat had reached the jetty and landed the remainder of the rifle company who were quickly establishing a base from which they too flushed our snipers from the surrounding jungle. The frightened and relieved hostages were shepherded into a cell in the police station while the marines established the building as their headquarters and hospital;. The bodies of the three dead marines were brought into the building and laid out on stretchers in one of the rooms adjacent to the cells. The body of Metcalf remained on board the landing craft covered in a combat jacket.

Now, the two machine guns were of little use as the rifle company was all over the area and to use them could mean hitting their own troops; so one was put ashore on the jetty and covered the south end of the town while the other was kept at a state or readiness on the second boat.

A message reached the boat that the medic ashore needed another stretcher at the hospital in a hurry.

"Lewis, get a stretcher over to that big building over there on the double" yelled Baron.

"Shit. Why me?" From the comparative safety of the boat, Lewis was not keen to move.

"Just get yer arse mobile" said Baron in an unusually stern voice. Lewis leapt overboard onto the jetty, a sub machine gun in one hand, the stretcher in the other and half crawling, scampered across the boards, jumped a ditch and dashed across the road into the makeshift hospital.

"One stretcher for the use of....." he panted. "Oh Christ."

Seeing the three dead bodies laid out before him, Lewis felt suddenly weak at the knees and sank to the floor on his haunches. Next to him was another body, blood oozing from a gaping wound in the chest and running down the sides onto the concrete floor where it lay in a pool. A Naval medic subjected the body to every test before declaring the marine dead.

"Give me a hand to get him on your stretcher Lewy" asked the medic

"OK." Rising from his squatting position Lewis then bent down to grasp the marine's legs. As he did so a burst of bullets smashed into the wall above him at head level scattering concrete and dust all over him and the medic and the bodies. The bullets had been accurately fired through the small slats used as windows in the station.

"Fucking hell. Stay down everybody, so they're still around."

As he finished speaking the Commander of L Company scuttled into the room. "Ah, Lewis. Just the man."

"Jesus, now what?"

"Look at this map Lewis"

"What's this, the Red Light district?"

"Don't piss about; this is serious in case you've forgotten. Those poor bastards are not play acting." he nodded towards the bodies.

"Sorry sir."

"Right then. This is where we are" he said pointing to a spot on the map which Lewis easily identified. "Just along here are the streets we are about to clear, running at right angles to the river. I want you to get back to the boat and get your machine guns mounted on the starboard side and position the boat opposite these streets where we'll be clearing the houses. They've all got big shutters on the windows, so when we've cleared a house we'll throw open the shutters and you'll know it's cleared. When you see the shutter open, put a burst into the very next house, just for a few seconds only as we'll be straight in there. Is that understood?"

"Yessir. I think so."

"You're not paid to think; just get a bloody move on. We'll wait until we see the boat move off before we start. Go."

"Bugger me, that bloody jetty seems farther away than when I left it" thought Lewis as he raced back to the craft, imagining the spasmodic firing he heard at the other end of town was solely aimed at him. Without incident he reached the boat and flung himself over the side lying panting on the deck.

"Where's Baron?" he gasped. "Tell him I've got a message from L Company CO that he'd better act on a bit smartish." Baron was called and the details explained to him.

"Right lads; get the guns and ammo over to the starboard side. Keep the tripod legs weighed down with these bags of empty cylinders."

"You don't waste much time do you, Sarge?"

"Could be a few bobs worth here" he smiled patting a bag of spent cylinders. "The good Lord provideth, my 'ansomes....."

"How did Hitler miss him?"

"I'll be on the bridge lads and I'll direct the fire from there."

Jock Mackay was delegated by the Baron to become the first engineer and sent below to start the engines. Baron figured that as Mackay had once worked in a garage he was the automatic choice.

"Cast off forward; cast off aft." Baron commanded leaning out of the bridge cabin.

"Thinks he's Captain Birdseye now" grinned Lee.

"He's happy. leave him alone, he'll play for hours." said Laker settling behind the other machine gun, just six feet separating the two.

"Tally-ho my hearties. A life on the ocean wave. Just the ticket." cheerily shouted the enigmatic Baron.

"He's fuckin' bombed-out" laughed Linden.

Positioning the craft some twenty yards from the shore, they cut the engines and watched as the two foot patrols carefully approached the street they were to clear. As the rifle troops reached the first street they split into two halves and took one side of it each, so Baron ordered one gun to each patrol.

"You know the score, gunners, so look after your own patrol. Remember, don't fire until the shutters open."

The streets were empty and silent as the patrols positioned themselves ready to take their first houses. As was the standard procedure for house clearing, two marines, covered by the rest of the patrol stationed themselves each side of the bottom windows and on the given nod lobbed two grenades through the window and hit the deck. As soon as they exploded the door was kicked open and the room sprayed with automatic fire from their sub machine guns. Seconds after they had entered the room a body was unceremoniously kicked out of the door, down the large pavement step and into the dusty road.

"That's one bastard less. Give them time to get upstairs and open the shutter then we'll give them a burst next door." said Lewis

With that the other machine gun opened up on the other side of the street as the patrol carried out the same routine, but with no success. An hour, six bodies and fifteen captives later the Commander of the patrol had completed his task and signalled the craft to return to the jetty. Once there the two guns were ordered ashore to cover the south end of the town ready for the imminent arrival of the back-up troops that were expected at any time.

"Right-ho lads, give each gun a quick clean and oil up, but just one at a time. Don't want to be caught with our kecks down do we?" said Baron as usual smiling broadly.

"How many rounds do you reckon we've got through so far Scouse?"

"About eighteen liners worth I reckon. that's roughly 4500 rounds then, eh?"

"Yeah."

"Why?"

I just wondered why Baron was carting all those bloody sacks around.

"Now I know; but how the hell he'll flog that lot here, I'm buggered if I know."

"Have faith in your leader my sons. What the good Lord......"

"Yeah yeah, we know. C'mon let's get this gun on the ball."

As soon as the guns were cleaned and ready Baron gave the order to move them onto the jetty alongside the road which separated them from the newly acquired headquarters and the surrounding jungle. Directly opposite the jetty and twenty yards from the HQ rose a sharp, steep bank covered in thick foliage which at one time in the not too distant past had been hacked down but now had grown again to about four feet high. Behind them was the river and due south the far end of town where the road led into a few shacks and then very thick jungle. So the machine gunners were able to command an almost 180 degree arc of fire.

Just as they settled the guns into position there was one almighty bang. Seeming to come from absolutely nowhere. Everybody dived for cover totally bemused and bewildered as to the origin of the explosive sound.

"Hey! Get me out of this bloody water."

"That's Baron. Where the fuck is he?"

"I'm down here in the bloody water. Get me up."

"How the bloody hell did you get there Sarge? What was that bang"

"That was the poxy RAF. Two Hunters or jets of some sort obviously doing a straffing job to frighten the bleedin' rebels. Probably came over and broke the sound barrier at tree height."

"So how in hell did you get there then?"

"I'd just got off the bleedin' boat dived for cover the same as you lot, but I missed my footing and rolled down the bank into the river. Now stop fucking laughing and help me out. I bloody near drowned and I don't like the thought of bleedin' sea snakes sniffing round me parts. C'mon, hurry up."

Hauling Baron out was a difficult enough exercise but to do so without laughing was impossible, but afterwards no-one laughed more than the bedraggled Sergeant and this endeared him even more to his men.

Ordering the gunners back to their weapon, Baron squelched back onto the boat in order to get dried out.

"Shit, I wish I'd had a bloody camera, Scouse that was bloody funny. I damn near pissed myself laughing."

"Yeah, that was a classic."

"Hey, what's going on over at HQ?"

A large three-ton lorry commandeered by the rifle troop had drawn up outside the headquarters and eight captured rebels were pushed off the back and sprawled in the dusty road while another marine proceeded to kick three dead rebel bodies from the floor of the wagon. Rigor mortis having set in, the bodies bounced grotesquely as they hit the road.

"Right you bastards, start digging. Bury these buggers right here. Move!" said an NCO throwing picks and spades from a sack to the prisoners. The one reluctant rebel was soon persuaded to change his mind as one of his guards jabbed him in the back with the bayonet at the end of his rifle until blood seeped through his pale blue shirt.

Now the immediate area around the jetty appeared to be clear of insurgents the pressure eased a little. The bodies from the hospital were brought across to the jetty and placed on the machine gunners boat to await the arrival of the large Supply Landing Craft that was at the very moment rounding the bend in the river and heading towards them.

"Now, the blood and snot's stopped flying I expect that's our reliefs on board" hoped Lee.

"Just back up I reckon" said Lewis. "More ammo, stores, food and mail."

"No chance of you getting back to Singers for a while yet my 'ansomes" said Baron, resplendent in a huge pair of jungle green underpants and very little else. "I'd say you could count on another couple of months here at least."

"Nothing like a cheerful bastard to make the day complete, is there?"

Ten minutes later Baron assumed the task of guiding the SLC into the jetty and tying it alongside their boat across which the newly arrived troops struggled with boxes and crates of ammunition and supplies.

Difficult Decisions. Tragic Outcome

"Ere, whadda yuh think that dugout's up to upstream?" said Moran who was on watch on one of the guns.

"It's been going to and fro across the river for some time now." In the distance, about five hundred yards upstream , the dugout had just reached the bank opposite them and was unloading its occupants.

"Fuckin' hell" said Lewis on the other gun. "I reckon they're ferrying some rebels over to the other bank so they can come down this side and catch us in the act."

"Where's Baron?"

"Fuck Baron. I'm going to give them a few bursts. By the time he gets out of his kecks they'll be down here and we'll be in the shit. Whadda you reckon? 500 yards?"

"Yeah, about that. Trial and error I guess."

Setting his sights accordingly, Lewis fired the standard four second burst; one banana, two banana, three banana, four.

"You're over the top. Drop fifty."

"What the bloody hell's going on?" yelled Baron racing from the boat. What the hell are you firing at?"

"That dugout Sarge. It keeps going backwards and forwards across the river and we think they may be trying to catch us in some crossfire by coming down the other bank."

"Yeah, could be I guess. Give them another burst if they go back again. I'll check your fall of shot."

Fear at the realisation they had entered a real theatre of war was evident on the faces of the newly arrived troops as they warily continued the task of unloading the SLC.

"Could you see how many were in it last time Lewy?"

"Three or four I think. Couldn't tell if it was blokes or not though."

"Don't worry about that my son; just as easy for a dame to pull a trigger."

"C'mon you little bastards, just one more time. I'll let it go back if it's empty, then get it again if it returns."

Moments later the dugout returned to the same bank they were on with only one occupant.

Smoothly lining up the sights of the gun on the now stationary boat, Lewis perspired as he waited for it to move out into the river, the beads of sweat running into his eyes and down his face until the droplets fell from his chin. His clammy hands firmly gripped the gun as his eyes strained to see the slightest movement ahead of him. Then, at last, the small dugout edged away from the bank and out into the river.

"Hang fire; wait until it's a bit further."

"Come on, come on. Just a bit further."

"Hold it, hold it, OK Fire!"

With devastating accuracy a hail of bullets ripped into the tiny vessel and its occupants one of whom Baron could make out through his binoculars was now grotesquely hanging over the side in death.

"Got the bastards" yelled an elated Lewis.

"Quick, get one of those dinghies out into the river and pick it up as the current brings it down" ordered Baron. "Cover the dinghy from both guns and keep an eye on the far bank just in case."

The shot up vessel was now progressing towards them steadily in the strong flowing river, keeping almost uncannily in the middle.

"Steady lads, steady," called Baron "OK they've got it. Bring her in lads" he shouted to the three rifle company men who had by now lashed a rifle sling to the dugout and were towing it to the bank. The grim expressions on the faces of the marines bringing the dugout to shore told the watching troops that all was not quite right, and, as it finally reached the bank the awful reality of their action hit those standing by smack in the face, for in the frail craft, cut to ribbons by the machine guns bullets were the remains of a man, a woman and two small children. Not a weapon in sight. and not a prayer of life.

"Bloody 'ell."

"Jesus."

"Get the poor bastards out and over to that mass grave they're digging" ordered the ever practical Baron.

"Fucking hell. What've I done?" said Lewis who had now joined the group standing around the pathetic scene, the realisation and horror so evident on his face, as he sweated and trembled, close to tears.

"Lee, get down below with Lewy while we sort this out and stay with him. I'll be there in a minute. The rest of you get back to your stations and carry on. Get those stores over to the headquarters on the double!" he barked.

Baron had not wanted the sight of what lay before them to stick in Lewis's mind but there was no doubt that was an impossibility, so to get him away from the scene as soon as possible was paramount and with his close buddy Lee, there was at least a hope that he could be partly convinced that it was all in the line of duty and not his fault. Seemingly only hit twice but both times in the head, the boy between the eyes and the beautiful young girl, both aged about ten, through the temple, the contorted figure of the woman next to them by comparison was more distressing. Almost cut in half, all that kept the lower part of her body attached to the top was a small piece of flesh at her hip. The rest was missing.

And the man. The back of his head was completely blown out and was now probably providing nourishment for a sea snake or fish, for it was certainly not visible to the marines.

Having organised the removal of the bodies and the cleaning of the blood spattered dugout and the surrounding area where the bodies were dragged ashore, Baron headed down below to Lewis and Lee. Lewis had been physically sick twice and was shaking like a leaf. Shock had set in and Baron knew that he must now draw on all his experience and resourcefulness to get Lewis right again as soon as possible.

"Look my son, don't feel so bad. You could've been exactly right and half of us could be under a white sheet like our mates out there. Once, when I was in Cyprus during the emergency a woman came towards me at a road block we'd set up, with her hands behind her back. I shouted to her in the local lingo and in English to stop, but she didn't. I kept on shouting but it made no difference. She just kept on coming. I thought she had a grenade or bomb behind her back, because it had happened before out there. Sort of Kamikaze patriots that didn't care if they died or not. So I shot her stone dead right there and then. There was nothing behind her back. No grenade. No bomb. Nothing. Later I found out she was deaf and dumb. So I really

37

do know what you're going through my son. Just got to look at it as an act of war that you were ordered to carry out. Not your fault at all."

"But the kids; their faces. It was terrible....."

"I know, I know. You won't forget it, but try and shove it to the back of your mind and get on with life as it comes."

"It was fuckin' horrible."

"Yeah, I know. Come on, get a brew down you and get back to the gun when you're ready."

"Stick with him Scouse. Come up when you like, OK?"

"Right-O- Sarge."

"Are they................have they been..........?"

"Yeah, the lads buried them in a separate grave, It's all over now. Try and get on as normal, kid." said Mackay sympathetically.

"That was bloody awful. I can't' forget the sight of their bodies, especially the kids."

"Yeah, me too. But this ain't no exercise. The Baron's right, it could just as easy be us that got buried." said Moran.

"I suppose so. Gotta try and shove it to the back of my mind, but it's bleeding difficult."

Limbang Security

66What's those lads up to up there?" said Luther, pointing up to the bank in front of them where a small group of the rifle company was attacking a position barely a hundred yards from them.

"Man the guns, quick" called Baron. "If anything moves put a burst through it."

After a short encounter in which no life was lost, two figures stood up out of the undergrowth raising their hands as they did so while the rifle troop surrounded them and eventually took them captive.

"Bloody hell! How long've they been there?" exclaimed Laker in his most expressive Wolverhampton drawl.

"Christ knows. But the bastards could've picked us off any time they felt like it from that range" said Lee.

"Shit; what if they'd had a few grenades? We'd have been blown to buggery and back" said Lewis as Baron nodded agreement whilst quietly congratulating himself that his theory that the sooner Lewis got back into the swing of things, the quicker he would push his bad experience to the back of his mind, proved correct; at least for the moment.

"With all the muck and bullets we've thrown around, you'd have thought they would have scarpered long ago" threw in Mackay as an afterthought.

"Probably too shit scared to move once we landed."

"Wonder if there's any more around?"

"Fuckin' 'ope not" said Moran. "The lads'lls do a sweep through there now just to make sure anyway" he concluded.

By mid afternoon Limbang itself was completely under the control of the marines, those rebels having survived the attack either fleeing into the jungle or been taken captive or shot. The killing of fifteen rebels had cost five Royal Marine lives. But many of the fleeing rebels had been badly injured and it was odds on that very few would make the safe Indonesian border before dying from their wounds.

Earlier, a group of nine local people had been herded onto the brow of the gunner's boat ready for transfer to the larger craft and passage to Brunei for reasons the marines were unaware. Returning from delivering a message to the headquarters, Luther brought with him a rumour that one of the group had been responsible for the death of two marines.

Lewis snapped.

Leaping from the gun position and grabbing his sub machine gun in one movement, Lewis raced for the landing craft shouting "I'll kill that bastard."

"Lewy, come back you stupid sod" yelled Lee after his comrade as he too raced for the boat.

Baron heard the shout and appeared out of the bridge of the craft just as Lewis rushed past him towards the group. Quickly following him forward, he reached Lewis barely seconds after Lewis had decided the oldest man in the group was its leader and had firmly stuck the barrel of his SMG up the nostril of the shrivelled old man.

"You bastard, I'm gonna blow your fucking brains out. Grabbing his arm and moving the gun away from the furiously shaking man, Baron contrived to cool Lewis down. "Leave him alone, Lewy. He's old and no danger to us now."

"But this arseole's shot two of our lads; and I'm going to send him where he belongs."

"C'mon Baron; he deserves all he gets, don't you bastard?"

"Get off him."

"Please let me have him, please! Just one shot up his nose, that'll do. They won't miss one less."

"Put that safety catch on Marine Lewis and get back to your gun position."

"I want him Sarge, badly"

"Forget it; if they're in the shit they'll get what's coming to them one way or another."

"They'd fucking better, the bastards. I've had my fill of these arseole's, the sooner I get back to UK the better."

"I couldn't agree with you more" said Baron steering the young marine back to the bridge.

Shortly afterwards the word was spread that the immediate town of

Limbang was now under a 24 hour curfew even though it was believed that the remaining rebels had all left the area. The power station and the government offices were all under the marines' control and apart from those on guard duty or patrol, all could stand down for a few hours.

The two machine guns were pulled back to the SLC and the platoon was bunked down on their own smaller craft, which met with their hearty approval for not only did they feel infinitely safe on board but it was good that they were together on their own, away from the hassle of the Headquarters.

The night passed without incident and bright and early next morning the platoon was called upon to weigh anchor and from the river cover a small kampong, a few hundred yards up river while a foot patrol searched the dozen or so huts for arms or ammunition. This prove a fruitless exercise but eased them back into the awareness of their situation.

The Provider

When they returned to the jetty orders were issued that due to the minimal amount of food supplies that the SLC had brought, they were now permitted to enter any of the stores in Limbang and take whatever was sufficient for their immediate needs with the proviso that a chit signed by the senior rank would be left with the owner of each store to cover the eventual payment of any items taken.

"Come on my 'ansomes," beamed Baron. "This is where we dip in."

"Whadda ya mean Sarge?" asked Laker.

"I mean my old son that this where we get that fucking boat stocked up with all the goodies we can get our hands on, and all for sweet Fanny Adams."

"How's that then Sarge?"

"Just get your weapon handy and grab Lewis and follow me" Baron answered Lee. "This could be a bloody sight better than Tesco's on a Saturday morning.

"Where are we going to then?" asked Lee.

"Just follow me my sons. Oi, Taffy bach, slow down a sec." Baron flagged down a passing wagon driven by a weasel like, thin Sergeant from the rifle company. "Where are you going with the motor?"

"Back to HQ"

"Nice motor; where'd you get it ?"

"Found it outside a sort of factory up the road, why?"

"Taffy, my old sunshine, how would you like a nice drink on your old Uncle Baron?"

"Whadda you up to now?"

"Taffy, have I ever let you down?"

"No, but...."

"OK then; first give us a lift up the road and then lets' suppose you were just having a slash in a doorway when somebody just happened to borrow your wagon for a half hour or so. No one would be the wiser would they?"

"No, don't suppose they would. but...."

"No need to thank me Taffy back; Hop in lads. You'll be well rewarded my old sunshine. Forward!"

"How does he bloody do it?" said Lewis.

"Years of practice, my son, years of practice."

The illustrious Baron had, from the jetty, been keeping a sharp watch on the largest building amongst the row of apparent stores that lined the street. This one was brightly painted in a new coat of paint which, by Baron's logic, meant that the owner was making enough money to be able to afford such a luxury and therefore it was a fair bet that the pickings from there would be the most lucrative.

Bringing the wagon to a halt ten yards from the front of the building Baron ordered Lee and Lewis out while the hapless Welshman was directed towards the Headquarters in the opposite direction.

"OK lad, don't take any chances. One each side of the door and I'll do the talking."

"Makes a change" grinned Lee.

Grinning also, Baron rapped loudly on the door, "Open up, open up. Come on, hurry up."

"OK, OK, I comin' Johnny."

Bolts were slid back from the inside as a babble of excited voices confirmed that there was more than just the male voice which answered in the building, so it was with extra caution that the marines awaited the opening of the door. Finally it swung open and a small and very frightened Malay appeared.

"You want something Johnny?" the trembling voice asked.

"Yeah; food, beer and anything else worth having. Time for you to look after your liberators. Inside, boyo."

"Plenny food Johnny. Plenny Tiger. Plenny drink."

"Where?"

"You come Johnny. You come."

"Careful Scouse, he could be taking you for a little walk into something nasty."

"I doubt it" replied Lee. I've got my SMG stuck right up his arse."

Leading through to a back room they came across the owners of the other voices they had heard. The rest of the family they correctly assumed, were all huddled into a corner of the room; two women and three small children. Lewis started to shake and sweat profusely but Baron, seeing what was happening immediately said "Christ, look at this lot; they've got more than bloody Tesco's. C'mon Lewy, get some of this gear into boxes and load it on the wagon. Make a bee-line for those tins of crab and prawns and those tins of pork and beef. We'll eat like kings tonight."

"They won't have more than Tesco's for long. Here, you , get some boxes and load up all I tell you to" he called to the owner.

"Yes Johnny. Me velly quick."

"You fucking better be. I ain't in the mood for no crap from any bastard right now."

"Steady, Lewy, he's shitting himself as it is" came the steadying influence of Baron. We'll take all the canned stuff only. I don't trust that fresh gear. Probably get foot and mouth" he laughed.

"So where's all the booze then?" Lee asked of the owner.

"What is booze Johnny?"

"Tiger, beer, whisky, brandy, you doughnut. Where is it?"

"Me find, Johnny, me find."

"You'd better try bleeding hard sunshine. Don't give me the slightest excuse to blow your fuckin' brains out."

"Take it easy Lewy" said Lee "Come on, let's get after him and see what's at the back of this place."

"Here Sarge, come and look at this little lot" called Lee as they squeezed through a narrow entrance to a back room.

"Jesus" said Baron as he eyed the shelves full of bottles of most of the recognised brands of spirits and the crates of Tiger beer stacked on the floor. "There's enough to sink the bloody Navy. C'mon lads, let's get as much of this stuff on the wagon as we can and get going; don't want no bastard catching us with this lot, eh,?"

"We'll have to stow it all below decks, Sarge, else some bugger will blow the gaff on us."

"Yeah. We'll worry about that when we get back. Get the owner to help you load up and I'll watch the rest of the gang."

"Bloody typical"

"I'm in charge......"

"Couldn't take charge of his prick if he had to" murmured Lewis out of earshot.

"For Christ's sake snap out of it Lewy. Just let's get this stuff on the wagon and back to the boat, then we can have a fuckin' good drink and stuff ourselves rotten. I'm bleedin' starvin"

"Yeah, OK. Things going through my bloody head at the moment, that's all."

"You don't have to tell me. I know. I'm the same, but what's done is done and there's sod all you or anyone can do about it now, so we've just got to get back on the ball. Just try and shove it to the back of your mind. And besides, we're due for repat, remember? So it can't be long now, right?"

"OK buddy. Right then, back to the boat for a skinful it is."

With the aid of the owner, mostly the aid of the owner, the wagon was filled with as much as they could carry without advertising their cargo.

"Heh Johnny, me want chitty."

"Balls. S'pose we'd better give him one. Might want some refills later. Got any paper anyone?"

"Only shithouse paper Sarge"

"That'll do. Give it here."

"Right, here you are Jock. One chitty."

"He looks like a stroppy little Scotch git don't he ?"

"Yeah. How long has your name been Irvine then Sarge?"

"Ever since that little bastard provost Sergeant dropped me in the shit. About time he paid for it."

"Espirit de Corps, ain't it?"

"Share and share alike my 'ansomes. He'd do the same for me if the little bastard got the chance. Let's go."

"Shit, what the bloody hell's up with this thing?" Baron cursed as not a spark of life emitted from the wagon.

"Sounds like the starter to me."

"Nobody got a spare on them I suppose......."

"Not just now. Fuck it."

"Now what?"

"Hang fire, there's a wagon coming down the road now. We'll

45

hitch a lift."

"But they'll tumble what we're up to and want a cut....."

"Leave it to me my son." said Baron flagging down the three tonner that approached and smiling as he saw he outranked the rifle troop corporal that was driving. "Hold on there Corporal. Got a bit of a problem here. Need your assistance."

"What's up Sarge?"

"Need a lift back to the jetty, OK?"

"We've got some cargo in the back that has to get to HQ soonest." replied the Corporal.

"What's that then?"

"Prisoners"

"How many?"

"Half a doz"

"Well , they're not going anywhere are they?"

"No, but....."

"Get them down here then; I've got some vital supplies that are desperately need at the jetty. CO's orders."

"Only two are alive though; well, they were when we picked them up."

"They'll do. Get them down here on the double my ansome and unload these supplies." an authoritative edge to Baron's voice.

"Right away Sarge. OK hop down and give the Sergeant and his lads a hand."

Leaping from the truck, three marines crossed to the wagon and began unloading the supplies at Baron's direction.

"Did someone say these supplies were vital?" asked one of the riflemen.

"What's so vital about beer and brandy?"

"Purely medicinal. Absolutely essential for troops in a state of shock."

"What's with all this food and booze, anyway?" asked the Corporal.

"Where is it going exactly?"

"Very important mission coming up said Baron taking the young Corporal to one side, "Very hush hush" he said winking. "Involves the landing craft and this stuff must get on board as soon as possible.

COs orders. Understand me?" winking again.

"Right O Sarge. Sorry didn't realise. C'mon you lot, get this stuff on board at once."

With total disregard the supplies were loaded on the truck on top of the four dead bodies that lay within.

"Christ, you lot have had a field day, haven't you?" said Lee.

"Yeah. They were in the fish market at the end of town. Tried to surrender, but we just shot the bastards. Got a taste for it after a while, don't you?"

"You might" said Lewis.

Baron climbed into the front of the truck with the Corporal while Lee and Lewis clambered into the back with the others.

"Hey Sarge," called Lee, "What are you going to tell that other stripey about the wagon?"

"Damaged in action, my son; damaged in action." he laughed.

Foot and Boat Patrols

Back on board the boat the platoon enjoyed their first decent meal for a few days but were allowed only a limited supply of the drinks they had secured as Baron was called to an O Group and this suggested that they could be detailed for duty that night. This proved, to their disgust to be the case.

Baron's orders were to take a patrol along the bank of the river in the opposite direction from the town, at midnight, and try to determine just how many buildings were in the area and , if possible get an idea of the number of inhabitants. Though how the hell he was to do that in the dark, he had not a clue. But orders was orders and had to be obeyed!

"Right my lovelies, gather around and pin back yer lugs. This is our mission impossible for tonight."

"Ain't the CO ever heard of kip? I'm bloody knackered" said Laker.

"Don't worry, this will be a doddle. All we've got to do is go upstream a bit and see how many bashers are there and how many of our coloured friends are around. No problem, eh?"

"How are we to see in the dark? Light a bloody candle?"

"You're always eating bloody carrots aren't you? Well, let's see just how good your eyesight is then."

"Of course they're good for you." said Laker. Did you ever see a bloody rabbit wearing glasses?"

"Very droll, my son."

"OK then. Mac, you and Moran can stay behind on watch, but don't nod off for Christ's sake. We don't need anymore bollickings from bloody Robbo."

"OK Sarge; what time will you be moving out and what time can I expect you all back?" asked Mackay.

"We'll be leaving about midnight or thereabouts and we could be back in a couple of hours; there again we could be back in the early hours around dawn, depending on how we go on."

"Right, I was just thinking about having a brew ready for you

48

when you get back."

"Lying sod. All you're worried about is getting caught with your heads down."

"Who me Sarge?"

"Go on, sod off. And stay awake."

"What's the rig Sarge?"

"Usual. SMGs, ammo pouches, water bottle and blacked out. I've got hold of some cork so we won't have to use that stinking mud again."

"I reckon a couple of hours kip is in order. I'm off down below" said Luther heading for the stern of the boat.

"What I couldn't be doing in civvy street right now instead of playing bloody Audie Murphy games" he bemoaned. Since he'd enlisted, Luther had realised he'd made a mistake and had tried every scheme imaginable to get a discharge. Tall and blonde and lean with it, he had, in desperation even tried to con the Medical Officer when he was in hospital for a broken ankle that he was a homosexual but he ruined that plan by being caught in the bedding store with a young nurse, the pair of them wearing only a smile!

Laker on the other hand was big, dark and swarthy; as black as the Black Country he came from. Immensely likeable with his ready wit and Brummie accent, Laker was a useful man to have around in a scrap being a former Inter Services Middleweight Champion although once the ale flowed in his veins he'd tended to become slightly punch drunk and more than once had one of his colleagues been mistakenly clobbered in a fight.

"OK lads, get heads down now. Mac will shake us with tea at 2330 hours, won't you?"

"Of course. The silver service I assume?"

"But of course."

The brilliant moon that night was greeted with mixed feelings by Baron and his patrol. While it was easier for them to see exactly where they were going, by the same token it was easier for any adversaries to locate them; so it was with great care and concentration that they set out. For two hundred yards they followed the road alongside the river then cut into the jungle on a pre-set bearing to get behind the kampong which was their immediate objective. Edging their way

49

slowly through the now intensely insect ridden undergrowth their susceptibility to ambush was apparent to all and ears and eyes strained for the slightest unusual sound. With the spasmodic moonlight their only guide, progress was painfully slow and difficult but at last they came across the one tributary they had to negotiate on patrol. Luck was with them as, only a few yards from their position was a small bamboo bridge, the light shining off the smooth cane.

"One at a time and all round defence when we get over" whispered Baron. "And for Chrissake take it easy Laker."

Laker had a problem. Bridges. There could not have been a bridge in the whole of the Far East through which they had travelled or taken part in exercises, from which Lake had not fallen. He and his instructor had practised until they were blue in the face, but to no avail. His sense of balance completely vanished when he left the security of a bank. Lee, Lewis and Baron were all over without incident as Laker started across. Linden waited on tenterhooks for Laker to get over; it was no pleasure being the last man of a patrol, especially when the rest of that patrol was on the other side of a river, and at night. Cautiously Laker eased his way along the slippery bamboo slates until he was at last over halfway across. Then the inevitable. A lace from his jungle boot caught fast between the bamboo, and try as he might it just would not come free. In final desperation Laker gave one almighty tug with all his strength. The effort completely threw him off balance and with a resounding crash he fell headlong into the stream.

"Oh no! Not again."

"Shit shoot, Bloody Malayans. Can't they learn to build a proper bleedin' bridge."

Soaked to the skin Laker managed to drag himself to the bank still cursing every Asiatic mother's son.

"Shut up" hissed Baron from the far bank.

"I'm bleedin' soaked. Fuckin' stupid place to put a bloody bridge anyway."

"And you two can belt up as well" Baron directed at Lee and Lewis who were both in uncontrollable fits of laughter.

Meanwhile, on the other side of the bank Linden had decided he wasn't going to be stuck out on a limb any longer and dashed for the bridge. Now even slippier after Lakers' contribution, Luther had only taken two strides before he, too, in his haste missed his footing and crashed horizontally into the water.

"This is like something out of the bloody Beano" roared Lee.

Now even the Baron could see the funny side and as Lee and Lewis creased up with laughter he too beamed radiantly in the moonlight.

"It's alright for you bastards, we're fuckin' soaked. Let's go back now Baron. This is a bloody farce. Half of bloody Borneo must know where we are now."

"Hang about lads. Dry off as best you can. We might as well carry on now. You'll soon dry out. Besides, I've got to give the CO some information or he'll do his bloody nut again."

"But I'm squelching along like a bleedin' squad of Wrens on the march" Laker protested.

"Never mind; Soldier and Sailor too, as Rudyard would say."

"Well get bleedin' Rudyard to take my place then."

"C'mon lads, let's get going before it gets light. Silently, of course" grinned Baron.

"This is more like Fred Carno's bloody army each day."

"Different though, eh?"

"Bollocks."

In half an hour they reached the object of the patrol, a small semi-circle of bashers at the end of a prominent track they had followed. All appeared quiet in the small Kampong which consisted of just four huts about ten yards apart, which made it very simple for just one man from the patrol to cover the whole village while the others had a look around. Laker was designated the task, while the others would wait until dawn's first light before entering the nearest basher. As the sky started to lighten and the chorus of the animal and insect kingdom reached a crescendo Baron, Lee, Lewis and Linden crept forward to the nearest basher. Waiting at each side of the entrance for the slightest sound of breathing, the marines acknowledged Baron's signal that he was about to flash a light inside.

"Cover me." he whispered.

"Right."

The thin beam of light pierced the darkness inside the hut searching every corner while the others waited for the slightest excuse to let loose a few rounds into anything that moved.

"It's empty. Quick, everyone inside" breathed Baron.

Covering the windows and the entrance they were soon swallowed up in the darkness while outside nothing stirred.

"OK, that just leaves those three to check out; there must be some bugger around or there'd be no tracks."

"Shh! I heard something" whispered Lee.

Immediately they heard the rustle of feet on the ground outside and peering through the haze they watched a figure crossing from the basher at the far end of the kampong to the edge of the surrounding jungle. Then the familiar sound of water bouncing off earth.

"Yeah"

"Hey Sarge" said Lewis. "That basher next to us is really just a framework; looks like it's been burnt out sometime. So there won't be no bastard in there, eh?"

"Good thinking my son. So that just leaves the two at the end."

"Shall we split up or check them both out together?"

"I reckon it'd be better to stick together; that way we can cover the back and the front at the same time. Come on, let's go."

Silently the four crept over to the basher and once again the thin stream of light from Baron's torch searched the inside of the hut.

"This bugger's empty too."

"So they're all in the last one."

"Yeah. Probably the bloody orgy hut." he grinned. Signalling Lee and Lewis to position themselves to the side and rear of the one remaining hut Baron and Laker edged toward it from the front. Taking up a station each side of the door again they waited for sounds but none was forthcoming. They waited a few seconds then on Baron's signal he flashed the torch around the inside of the basher.

"Nobody move" barked Baron, at the huddle of bodies pressed together on the floor covered in old cloths and rags and bamboo prayer mats. Immediately the occupants sat bolt upright, the fear in their bright shining eyes very apparent as they broke out into a babble of excited, panicky chatter.

There were two women, three men and three small children all showing great fear and trepidation at the unexpected intrusion.

"Stay on the ground, face down" ordered Baron and to explain his order he placed his SMG in the back of one of the men's head, rolled him over and place a large size nine boot in the small of his back. The message was not lost and the others followed suit hugging the children to them in the process.

"OK lads, search the place; you know what we're after. And you two can shut up or I'll blow your heads off" he directed at the two women who were chattering furiously on the floor. By his tone, they understood.

Systematically they searched the basher from top to bottom but they found nothing of interest to them.

"There's fuck all here, Sarge" called Lee from the back of the hut.

"OK, we'll see. You, get up" he said releasing his foot from the small of the man's back. "Speak English?" he asked.

"Some, Johnny." replied the quivering old man.

"My name's bloody Baron not Johnny, OK"

"OK bloody Baron" repeated the man.

"Just Baron you doughnut, got it?"

"Yessir Baron. Me understand OK?" blurted the wizened old man, his face glistening in the half light as the sweat ran down it.

"And what are you lot laughing at now?" asked Baron as the remainder of the patrol saw the funny side of the interrogation. "Christ, we're trying to do some kind of a job here and all I get is Shakin' Stevens here and the bloody Gang Show. Get switched on my sons."

"Very good bloody Baron" mimicked Lewis.

"Oh, very droll" and turning to the man "Now you little sod where's the guns and ammunition stored?"

"No guns Johnny Baron; no bullets."

"Crap. You wanna see tomorrow?" snapped Baron pushing the barrel of the Sub Machine Gun against the nose of the trembling man. "Then tell me; where's the guns and ammo ?" yelled Baron in an unusually vicious manner which took the remainder of the patrol by surprise.

"No guns Baron sir; me very poor man." the man wailed, the

terror evident on his face.

Pointing to the nearest of the two women on the floor Baron asked "Your woman?"

"My woman. Very young. Very beautiful. You want?"

Ignoring the man, Baron barked "Get her up Lewis" at the same time removing his bayonet from its scabbard.

"Christ, what are you going to do Sarge?"

"I'll make the bastard talk. Laker, take the kids outside and stay with them. You two grab her arms and legs and hold her tight."

As soon as the children were out of the hut and the woman had ceased struggling in the marines' grasp Baron place his hand on the front of her sarong and in one swift downward movement ripped it to the waist exposing her firm young breasts. Ignoring the gasps of admiration from the others and the protestations of the man Baron grasped the nipple of her left breast and grotesquely pulled it away from her body as she screamed in pain. Then he placed his bayonet flat against her chest directly under her outstretched breast.

"Fuckin' hell Baron ...." started Lee.

"Shut up." snapped Baron. "Well you little bastard, what's it to be?"

"Me no guns Johnny sir; me speak truly."

Very slightly drawing the bayonet across the girls chest a thin red line of blood appeared and trickled down to her navel. "Your last chance my son or I'm gonna cut this bastard off; be a pity to fuck up such a nice your girlie, now wouldn't it."

"OK,OK I tell you where men keep guns. No me you understand, yes?"

"Get on with it."

Gesturing to the map case Baron carried, the coolie was obviously more intelligent than they had supposed and on receiving the spread out map proceeded to point to an area several miles away.

"Lookee, here are many caves. Men keep guns here. Me see long time."

"There'd bloody better be or I'll come back and blow your fucking head off sunshine. OK. found anything lads?" he called to Lee and Lewis who had been searching the hut meanwhile.

54

"Nah, fuck all."

"Right, lets fuck off then, Tie the adults to that centre post and let the kids loose in the ulu. We don't want the bastards creeping up behind us now, do we?"

Having secured the five adults in the hut and set the children free in the jungle, the patrol headed back to the track leading into the kampong. Just as they reached it a bullet whistled through the foliage above their heads; scattering for cover Baron yelled "Anyone see where that came from?"

"Yeah," said lee. "From that bloody basher we thought was only half built."

"Everyone OK?" asked Baron.

All were.

"Lee, Lewis get round the left side of the basher; Laker come with me to the right. Luther, cover us all. Move."

Crawling back deeper into the jungle undergrowth the two groups split and made their way to the target hut. Two further shots rang out as they slowly converged on the basher but they were wild and no danger at all to the commandos.

Then, just as Baron and Laker had crawled round to a position from which they could view the basher the muzzle of an old flintlock musket nosed its way out of the window and fired another shot in the direction they had just come from.

Lee and Lewis had also seen the barrel appear and had immediately raced to the basher and positioned themselves each side of the door, pulling the pins from two grenades as they ran with their teeth.

"Ready?" mimed Lewis.

Lee nodded and the two grenades hurtled through the window as the marines threw themselves to the ground. No sooner had they exploded than both commandos had kicked open the door and sprayed the inside the basher with bursts of automatic fire. Incredibly, in the corner of the hut lay a young man, still alive though cut to ribbons, covered in blood and groaning in agony on the floor.

"How the fuck did he survive that lot?" asked Lee.

"Christ knows."

"In a bit of a state, ain't he?"

"Not for long." One shot from Lee straight through the man's head ended his torment. "Oh shoot at us, bastard. C'mon, let's get out of here."

"You two OK?" called Baron.

"Yeah, no sweat."

Surveying the scene and ever mindful of the effect same could or might possibly have on Lewis, Baron said "C'mon, let's get back while the going's good. Half the bloody Borneo nation must've heard that lot. Get to the track and wait; I'll be right with you."

Minutes later the patrol headed back towards Limbang taking an alternative route to that they had come on; ' never use the same route - someone could be waiting for you' the manual had said.

After twenty minutes hard going through the thick jungle, made worse by the fact that they were climbing steadily, Baron came across a clearing and ordered a break and, with Laker on guard they sat down to rest a while. No sooner had they relaxed when Laker spotted a spiral of smoke coming from the direction from which they had travelled.

"Here lads, there's a load of smoke coming from the area of that kampong we were at. What do yuh reckon that is then Sarge?"

"Someone must've dropped a dog-end. C'mon let's go."

The following day the Commanding Officer held an 'O' Group to discuss the merits of the information submitted by the various patrols of the previous night and it was decided that a large patrol should investigate the caves Baron's patrol had been informed of. At 0700 hours the following day a 20 man group left Limbang and set out on the estimated four hour trek. A long hard slog ensued through varying degrees of terrain; thick jungle, scrub, paddy fields and many rivers and streams. Every member of the patrol at some stage had to burn the leeches from the visible part of his body whilst wondering just how many were on the not so visible parts. Laker contrived to fall off only two bridges in the whole of the outward journey which all agreed was something of a record and heartily congratulated him on this fine achievement.

"Piss taking bastards" was Laker's reaction.

At the head of the patrol Lieutenant Robson and CSM Punchy Nelson halted and signalled the patrol to take up all round defence while they moved on ahead to the prominent hill that rose before them as they eased their way out to the edge of the thick jungle.

"The caves should be at the top of this lot and round the other side, sir" said Nelson.

"Yes. Leave a small rearguard party and bring the rest up to me here ready for an advance to the caves."

"Very good sir" said Nelson as he scampered away the short distance to the rest of the patrol where he organised them accordingly.

Back at Robson's location the remaining men were split into two groups, each to advance on the caves from opposite directions in a classic pincer movement. "Rommel himself would have been proud of such action" mused Robson.........

Half an hour later after a particularly steep and strenuous climb, each man on tenterhooks expecting a confrontation of some sort, both sections converged at the same moment with impeccable timing on a small mound of rocks jutting out from the side of the hill. No more than five feet high, there was no possible way any amount , no matter how small, of arms could be hidden there and no trace was there of recent human activity in the area. In fact, had the rocks been any higher it was quite possible that both sections may have thought the other an enemy and a fire fight ensued.

"Sergeant Knight, you appear to have done it again" said an irate Robson, reflecting on the glory that might have been his.

"Is that it, sir?"

"Unless you can see anything else on this fucking hilltop that looks remotely like a bloody cave I suggest that yes, this is in fact, IT!"

"Well bugger me."

"Get the patrol together before I think of an even better suggestion, Sergeant. And I further suggest that you re-visit your source of information."

"That won't be necessary Sir. I took precautions if you get my drift. Couldn't have the buggers waiting here for us , could we?"

"I didn't hear that Sergeant. Move"

"Yessir."

57

Partly disappointed, greatly relieved and thoroughly exhausted the patrol finally reached their base at Limbang just prior to darkness falling. Their spirits were, however somewhat lifted on hearing that they(the MMG Platoon) had been designated a small agricultural office as a billet so removing their gear from the RCL they were able to bed down in much better conditions that night and after a fair meal of Irish stew and prawns washed down with a modicum of the local Brandy wine and a verse or two of Rudyard, they all slipped into oblivion.

The duties of the platoon for the next few days were restful, if boring. Their daily tasks comprised keeping the guns in top order, foot patrols around the town, the odd ambush at the fringe of the jungle on the edge of town and alternate nights with the Mortar platoon guarding the radio station situated at the far end of town next to a fish market. This duty was one they disliked intensely for the radio station was powered by a loud generator which was so noisy as to afford them no sleep at all during their watches.

In their off duty periods they all took great pride in relating their heroics to their kin in the endless letters they wrote; the culmination of their delight was to print at the top of their letters 'ON ACTIVE SERVICE' which they all felt sure was a certain bet to gain them a hero's welcome when they eventually did reach home.

One evening Lee had hit on the idea of writing to a prominent cigarette company telling them of the great pleasure and solace they enjoyed from smoking that company's produce, in the hope that, as they were British troops on active service, a host of free samples might ensue. The company failed to find such publicity of any constructive use, obviously, for they failed even to reply; but Moran on the other hand was slightly more successful. He wrote to a razor blade company saying how his blade had lasted for nearly two weeks in the torrid atmosphere of the Borneo jungle already and that it was still going strong! The company in reply thanked him wholeheartedly for his glowing tribute and sent him a further two weeks' supply - one blade!

Almost before they realised, Xmas eve was upon them and their thoughts naturally strayed towards home and their families. Baron had been through many Xmas's away from home and he contrived to do what he could to keep them occupied, even though he missed his own brood. He therefore decided to send the entire platoon out on a shopping expedition into town while he looked after the 'office' as he now referred to their billet. In brighter spirits Corporal Mackay and marines Lee, Lewis Luther, Laker and Moran set off for the centre of town.

An hour later found the platoon, staggering under the weight of two large blankets strung between them full of all manner of choice goods which they felt sure would appease their leader back in the 'office'.

Foolish Games

Congratulating themselves on their expedition success they decided that as it was indeed Xmas Eve and they had a night without duties it would not be unreasonable to call in at the only bar in the town for the odd 'wet' or two; so stowing their booty in one corner of the verrandah of the shack which acted as a bar of sorts, they squatted down on the floor while the only Malay in town permitted to waive the 24 hour curfew, served them. The verrandah comprised barely half a dozen small tables with two chairs to each so the majority of those engaged in their favourite pastime were sprawled untidily on the floor waiting until some left a chair vacant. Before too long the alcohol , heat and relaxed atmosphere led to a robust rendition of Xmas carols interlaced with the more raucous marine songs which all sang with great gusto.

The only exception to the happy scene was a confrontation between one of the Marines and the owner of the bar, who was most upset that his wife was happily sitting on the Marine's lap and obviously enjoying the attention. Trying to pull her away from the Marine prompted a physical response and soon both men were exchanging blows. However Mackay took charge and separated the two and sent the Marine out of the bar, and back to his section, the appreciation of the owner reflected in free drinks all round. Returning to their billet the Machine Gunners found their leader snoring profusely stretched out on his sleeping bag in a corner of the room.

"He'd be bleedin' useful for Securicor wouldn't he?" said Lee

"Let sleeping dogs lie."

"I'm not asleep; fully au fait and alert" drawled Baron struggling to adopt an upright position. "Everything's under control. Where's all the goodies then?"

"Want a beer Sarge?"

"Yeah, ta. What time is it? Where have you buggers been so long?"

"Bit of bother in that bar down the road, but other than that nothing exciting happened."

"S'pose I'd better get ready for the O Group. What's the time?"

"Six on the dot" "What time is O Group?"

"Quarter to si........ oh shit! "I'm going to be bloody popular again."

"Want a hand Sarge?"

"Christ, get out of my way everybody. Where's my bloody map case? Get my SMG and belt somebody, quick. Where's my beret? Oh sod I'm wearing it."

"Organisation , the best thing in the Corps........" mimicked Lewis.

"Bollocks. Open that bloody door, quick."

Scrambling through the door trying to tuck his shirt in his trousers and put his belt on at the same time, Baron headed for Headquarters and the meeting with the Commanding Officer.

Christmas Days

"Right my ansomes. Line up for your Xmas dinner and present all in one courtesy of Her Imperial Majesty's Government. And don't eat it all at once!" Baron handed each man a packet of Fox's Glacier Mints. "See how I looks after you all my sons?"

"You gotta be fuckin' jokin' Sarge."

"My son, there's three things I don't make funnies about - food. money and women. In that order. So either stuff these down your gullet or up your arse or give them to some bastard who will."

"Shave off. Is this what we pay bloody taxes for?"

"Remind me to write to my MP"

"How does one's body and brain survive on such a pittance?"

"If you 'ad a fuckin' brain you'd be dangerous."

"Anyway that's all we're going to get for now except for the wonderful news I've got for you about how you're going to spend your Xmas Day, so pin back your lugoles and listen. There's some kampongs where they think some bugger's stowing arms away and the AEs are going to paddle alongside our boat in dugouts, land and search these kampongs while we cover them with the guns from the river."

"Now, at 0900 we move off, so let's get our vital supplies loaded back on board ready for the off tomorrow. Moran and Ginge stay here and square this bloody mess deck off. The rest load stores."

"And have a brew ready for when we get back, suitably laced of course." called Mackay over his shoulder as they moved out of the billet.

Laden with as many supplies as each man could carry they set off for the craft, Baron keeping a wary eye out for anybody who might become inquisitive about their precious supplies, but nobody bothered them and they reached the boat without incident.

"We'll lock this little lot in the engine room so's no bugger can half hitch it in the middle of the night. Better give the old engine a quick turn over Jock just to make sure it's still on the ball, eh?"

"Ok Sarge, but keep that bloody whisky away from the diesel down below or it'll bugger it right up."

"Don't worry my son, I'll take care of it aright; can't have the bloody haggis wafflers up in arms can we lad?"

Having stowed their goods away, squared up the craft and tested the engines, Baron was satisfied that all was OK and they returned to the Agricultural office.

Duly at 1000 hours the next day the RCL edged its way from the jetty and proceeded to chug up river. The one hour delay in departure was caused by a member of the Assault Engineers putting a bayonet through the bottom of a dugout as he climbed into it and sinking it before it had left shore. Soon another was produced and all the stores transferred before they could all move off.

It was a beautiful morning, the sun shining brightly, birds and all the other jungle noises in profusion and the water as clear as glass as the RCL with two dugouts on each side slowly glided upstream towards the first kampong which, according to the map was only a mile away. However on reaching the location no kampong was to be found on either bank, so after a short stop to allow the AEs to get their breath back, Baron, proudly at the helm, decided to press on the two miles to the next kampong they were ordered to search.

Their course was against a fairly strong current, so it was not without some effort that the dugouts kept up with the RCL even though Baron could hardly have gone slower.

Gradually the crafts made their way upstream navigating the surprisingly hard bends in the river in quite a professional manner, Baron thought. He was in his element as skipper of the boat, strutting around the bridge checking everything and repeatedly, much to Mackay's annoyance, piping the engine room for progress reports on the state of the engines. Both he and the others were much enjoying the escape from the routine in Limbang on such a beautiful day, and very shortly they came across the next kampong set in a most picturesque location which enhanced their thoughts. A little bay set in the right bank surrounded by palm trees reaching extraordinarily high into the clear blue sky with the native bashers set in an almost perfect semi-circle around it to the waters edge. Now, the entire village had gathered at the small jetty on hearing the sound of the RCLs engines and an excited babble of noise greeted the AEs as they stepped ashore, fanning out into a defensive formation immediately in case of unexpected attack or ambush.

Showing absolutely no fear or trepidation at the sudden arrival of an armed military group, the natives continued their excited chatter as the AEs systematically proceeded to search each basher in turn looking for anything which might suggest enemy activity in the kampong.

"Look at the knockers on that one Jimmy. I'd give her one and no mistake." said Cannon , a big bawdy scot.

"I wouldn't touch 'er wiv yours. She's probably syphed up to the bleedin' eyebrows."

"But you'd crawl through your bloody granny if she gave you half a bleedin' chance" replied Sleeney, a rough, tough Irishman.

"Alright lads, there's fuck all here to interest us. Back to the boats." ordered Reid leading the patrol. "Cover our rear Smudge, I don't trust these bastards."

Carefully, they returned to the centre of the river, covered all the time by the ever watchful machine gunners on board the RCL. Lashing their dugouts to the side and after end of the mother craft, the AEs were hauled up onto the deck for a break.

"No joy Reid?" asked Baron

"Nah. Nothing much there at all. If there had been they'd have moved it out long before we got there. Nothing of any value around either so if they did have anything worth nicking they probably moved it all out into the bloody ulu somewhere and I wasn't going anywhere out of sight of the bloody machine gun."

"Fair enough my ansome" smiled Baron. "Park your arses anywhere you can and we'll get mobile."

"Where are we off to now, then?" asked Smith

"Xmas Day cruise" Baron grinned back at him. "Hold on to your lollipops my sons" With that he punched the button on the intercom and ordered Mackay to steam full ahead and the boat eased away from its mooring and cruised upstream through the crystal clear waters. Chugging around two more bends in the river, the boat was brought to a halt by Baron in a wider part surrounded by thick jungle on both banks.

"Are we going ashore here Sarge?" queried Reid somewhat disconcerted at the absence of a suitable landing spot. Baron assured him and the remainder that they were not and leaning out of the side of the bridge ordered Laker to relieve Lee on the machine gun and the rest to converge on him for a 'pow-wow'

"Right my ansomes. I promised you all a Xmas Day cruise and one you shall'ave We're going to anchor up here for a while and break out the goodies. A sort of floating ban-yan you might say. Now I just happen to have acquired this rather outsized radio so we've got music. The food and booze is all organised so all we really need is a boat full of virgins to come round the bend and we'll be all set" he laughed. "But as that's probably a bit too much to ask for we'll just have to sit here and dream about it, won't we?"

"How does he do it?" asked Bannon to no-one in particular.

"Organisation, my son, the best thing in the Corps."

"You never cease to amaze us 'O' Great White Leader" said Lewis

"OK then; one man on watch on the gun at all times just in case some bloody rebels stumble across us or the CO's on a scouting trip."

"More chance of Pompey winning the bloody FA Cup" called Lewis.

"Don't speak ill of the dead" laughed Baron.

"Come and fill yer boots then my 'ansomes. Xmas in sunny Borneo. Who could ask for anything more?"

"How about Xmas in bloody Honolulu with a pussers lawnmower?"

"Sex mad bastard."

"Tell us Sarge, how the bloody hell did you manage to get hold of all this clobber?" asked Reid.

"Listen, my son, when you've been in the mob as long as I have, the first thing you'll understand is that creature comforts come first no matter where you are. So you've gotta get organised. Organisation, the best thing in the Corps."

"Here we go again ...."

"The best part" continued Baron

"Is that we're not paying for it. If they take any notice of all the chits we've all signed in Limbang then bloody Levine will have to sign on for fuckin' life to pay for it all. Little bastard. Not often I call another NCO names but that guy is about as popular as a bacon sarnie in the Rabbi's lunchbox."

"Pour me a flagon of your finest ale, my barman" Lewis called to Lee who had quite naturally assumed the mantle of custodian of the liquor on the bridge.

"What do you think this is? Fuckin' Raffles?"

"That's the first place I'm going when we get back to Singers."

"I'm going to get as pissed as a fart and call all those stuck up officer's trash bitches every name I can think of" said Lewis. "They think they're the last bastion of the British Empire of fifty years ago. Get right up my fuckin' nostrils."

"They're all gettting shafted by each others' husbands too; and we get a bollocking for bagging off down Nee Soon. It ain't right. Roll on the bleedin' Revolution. I'll put them all in the Other Ranks brothel I'll open."

"They'd fucking love that."

"Yeah, but I'll make them get a pull through with a fuckin' fir tree."

"Nice bloke, ain't he?"

"And so subtle with it."

"Talking of brothels" said Lewis "do you remember that night we were on shore patrol together down the Larong Six district Scouse? When we went in that brothel with that rookie Army sub-lieutenant and caught Tug Wilson on the job, pissed as a newt?"

"Yeah, that was the first night run ashore after a month up the jungle school in Jahore Bahru. Old Tug was rampant as usual and knocking ten out of this slag when in we walk with this pongo pig shouting and farting all over the place. He saw Tug at it and started jabbing him in the back with his bleedin' cane."

"Just about the worst thing anyone could do to Wilson. He went fucking bananas."

"Yeah. This pig was saying in his Oxford accent 'get off her my man, filthy harlot; you're out of bounds you know young man; disgusting creature"

"Tug slowly climbed off this party, grabbed the pig and threw him on the bed; then he took his cane and forced the pigs mouth open and stuffed the cane as far down his throat as he could. I thought the pig was going to die. His eyes stood out like fuckin' golf balls. He couldn't move a muscle; well, you know the size of Tug...."

"In the end we had to pull him off, unfortunately and hustle him out of the brothel bollicky buff carrying his clobber. We told the pig when he eventually recovered enough that Tug had run off down an alley and we had lost him. Fuckin' sure he knew we were bull shittin' but in his state he wasn't exactly interested. We had to take him to BMH and they kept him in for a couple of days apparently. Lacerations of the throat."

"Tug's a vicious bastard when he gets going." chipped in Laker.

"We were in Hong Kong once in the China Fleet Club, at the same time as the bloody Sixth Fleet and the Kiwis, and there was Tug and this gionormous Kiwi matelot sitting at this table as drunk as arseoles staring at each other. They sat there for about twenty minutes saying bugger all, just keeping themselves upright with one arm apiece on the table. Then all of a sudden Tug put his hands on the front of the gorilla's square-rig and pulled like fuck. The whole lot came away in his hands and this Kiwi just stared at Tug for about five minutes. Then he looked at the remnants of his uniform, stood up and nearly touched the ceiling, leant across the table and with one hand grabbed Tug and threw him right across the room scattering a few hundred drinks in the process. 'Course the place was then in an uproar; every bastard piled in and there was one almighty punch up. Fuckin' MPs and Snowdrops all over the place. Anyway, next thing there's Tug and the gorilla stood side by side taking on all comers; big 'oppos. Took twelve MPs and Yanks to get the pair of them into a meat wagon."

"Then there was the time he got caught screwing the Padre's daughter. Yeah, really. She was a right randy cow. Rough as fuck, but white for all that. Tug was on duty watch at the officer's quarters one night and he chatted her up at a piss up they had. She was as pissed as a newt apparently. No-one could work out why he kept volunteering for duty up there, but she would sneak him into the padre's changing room in the church - -whadda ya call it? Vest room or something?"

"Vestry you arseole"

"Oh yeah, that's it. Anyway, he was knocking ten bells out of her there one night when in walks the fucking padre, bible in hand, wondering what the bloody lights are doing on. Silly cow left the door ajar. Tug reckons he fell to his knees praying aloud like fuck, so he did a quick bunk while she was pulling her kecks up. He was lucky though. All he got was a bollicking from the CO. Mind, everyone and the CO had been there too. Except the fuckin' padre. And he was as queer as a nine bob note."

"I expect Wilson's bagging off somewhere in Singers now, drunk as a fart and celebrating Xmas a bloody sight better than we are."

"Talking of Hong Kong reminds me of two buggers who very nearly spent the rest of their days inside for desertion, doesn't it you two?" said Baron eyeing Lee and Lewis.

"Oh yeah. We were bloody lucky that time, eh, Scouse."

"Too right. Mind you, I always fancied a cruise on a luxury Trans-Atlantic liner."

"What happened there then?" asked one of the AE's.

"Shit, well, grinned Lewis, me and Scouse were ashore from the Bulwark which was tied up at the jetty on Hong Kong island and we caught the ferry over to Kowloon on the Chinese mainland one afternoon. We did just about every bar in town and got well pissed. Then we decided to bring ourselves round with a sauna and massage at one of these exotic parlours, full of Chinese dolly birds - or so we thought. Anyway, we had all the hot and cold water treatment from some old geezer, then he told us to lie on the slabs of this fuckin' great bath and wait for the masseur. Well, we thought this is it , now for the birds. We must've laid there for about ten mutes getting really randy at the thought of it, when in walks this bloody great Samurai wrestler built like a brick shit house and proceeds to knock ten bells out of us!"

"It was more like a Chinese torture than a massage" added Lee

"But we felt bloody great after it. Fit as fuck."

"So what the bloody hell has that got to do with luxury liners?"

"Hang fire, I'm coming to that now. Well, we came out of there on cloud nine and reasonably sober, so we decided to lash ourselves up to a good nosh up. We found this real smart hotel with a superb restaurant and stuffed ourselves rotten on just about every delicacy on the me and you. Anyway, afterwards we naturally wound up in the hotel bar and started pissing up. We were about the only bastards in there apart from a charming little Chinese girl that Scouse was trying to get stuck across but she didn't want to become a Chinese takeaway so we were just seeing off our Tiger when in walks these two gorgeous bits of white trash and plonks themselves down next to us at the bar and starts chatting. We couldn't believe our luck. So it turns out these two birds are on a world cruise on the Canberra which incidentally, was tied up on Kowloon side. It was unbelievable. Not only fuckin' good lookers but loaded with it. So, using all the initiative bestowed upon us as Royal Marines, we said we'd show them the sights and off we went on a luxury crawl of the best hotels and bars in Kowloon, having, naturally, said that they were sorry that we were unable to show them around because we were on our last couple of bucks before payday; knowing that we were onto a good thing. Money was no problem with them and they really lashed us up something rotten, Taxis everywhere, all the booze we could handle and another fuckin' great meal later on. Anyway as you might expect, we naturally took it for granted that we were going to get stuck into these two in some smart hotel for the night, but they had other ideas. They shared a cabin on the ship and invited us back there. So with a great deal of persuasion......"

"Yeah, OK"

"It was bloody magnificent on that ship, eh Scouse?"

"Bloody right. Made Bulwark look like a bloody sanpan."

"They just rang this bell for anything we wanted and this steward was there in seconds. They even had their own bar, well stocked too, in the corner."

"Not for long it wasn't."

"Right. And I'm sure that steward was crawling through your one."

"I couldn't have given a fuck at that stage."

"Me neither. So we were kipped down with these two after a good session and a long run ashore and we slept like bleedin' babies. Anyway, I can't remember what time it was, but the first thing I knew was Scouse here shaking me in a bloody panic and shouting to lookout the damn porthole. So I looks out and what do I see? Only the bloody Bulwark passing by on the other side of the bleedin' harbour. Only Bulwark was still bloody tied up alongside. It was us that was on the bloody move."

"Yeah, those silly bitches had forgotten to mention the little fact that the fuckin' ship was leaving for bloody Western Australia that morning,. So it looked like we were going with them."

"So what did you do then?"

"Your mean apart from shit ourselves?"

"Well , for a start we contemplated wringing their fucking necks."

"They thought it was bloody funny. That was until we got on the phone to the bloody Purser."

"Went straight to the top then?"

"Well, it was him and the bloody Captain driving the thing, so who else?"

"Correct."

"So we got a quick shower and smartened ourselves up a bit and trooped off to find the bugger after a couple of good wets for breakfast of course."

"Yeah, couldn't leave all that booze just lying there." said Lee.

"We didn't quite know what to say to the sod but in the end we decided to fling ourselves at his mercy and told him the truth; without mentioning any names of course."

"Well, we'd had a bloody good run ashore on them so it didn't seem right to drop them in the shit, eh?"

"No. Anyway, the Purser marched us up to the skipper and luckily he turned out to be a good hand as well. The ol' man wasn't too happy, understandably , but he saw the funny side of it and figured we'd be in enough shit as it was. So he slowed the bloody ship down, lowered a lifeboat and ferried us right across the harbour to Bulwark's jetty. As we left the ship, all the passengers were still lining the decks looking at the scenery and they cheered like fuck when we set off.

"Yeah. The buzz must've got around bloody quickly."

"And all we got for being adrift was seven days number nines, which, as we spent the next ten days at sea on the way to bloody Aden for an exercise, was a fuckin' doddle."

"You lucky bastards."

"The devil looks after his own."

"Have you had any lucky escapes Sarge?" asked Lee.

"One or two. Like the time Palestine was on. We had to do a guard duty on a warehouse full of the rebel Army's supplies and me and this other corporal unscrewed the hinges on this door in the middle of the night, loaded all the gear we could muster on a Land-Rover, drove into the old town and flogged the bloody lot to some storekeeper. Luckily, we were moved out the next day and we found out later that the bloke we flogged the gear to had been raided the next day by the local gestapo and got locked up for bloody life for stealing.

"You got more jam that Hartley's."

"The good Lord provideth."

"Well, provideth me with another ale, landlord."

"Catch."

"Talking of bloody Levine, which we wasn't, do you remember that time at Lympstone when he was duty provo in the guardhouse and we buggered his motor up, Lewy?"

"Yeah, we certainly had the bastard then."

"Yeah. He'd parked his old Morris 1000 outside the back of the guardroom, the doughnut, so when he got his head down we sneaked round the back, jacked his car up, took all the wheels off and left it on a pile of bricks. He leapt out the guardroom the next morning, still in the dark cos it was winter, jumped into his motor and tried to drive off. Course, the whole fuckin' lot collapsed in a big heap and he had to get a garage out to get it fixed up."

"Not only fucked him about, but cost him a few bob, too."

"Little bastard."

"I never laughed so much since granny caught her tit in the mangle."

"Yeah, he went bloody spare. Called in the police, everything."

"Mind you, he couldn't prove bugger all and the coppers had a bloody good laugh too."

"Changing the subject" said Reid, "What time are we going back, Sarge?"

"No panic, squad. This is supposed to be an all day job and.....what the bloody hell was that?"

"Man overboard!" shouted Moran. Then, "Oh, it's not a man, it's Laker. That'll teach you to stand on the gunwhales and piss over the side, my son."

"Well, it's one way to cool down" shouted Laker splashing away quite merrily until someone reminded him that the river was full of the deadly sea snakes.

"Shit. Get me out of here. Throw me a line some bugger.

"Shall we lads?" Let's think about it over another beer."

"Now, if we leave him there, we won't have no bugger falling off bridges all the time, will we?"

"True, and it'll be one less to share the beer with" said Lee.

"That's a thought.............."

"C'mon you bastards, get me out of here."

"Ok lads, haul him out" ordered Baron, beaming. "Rig up a line so's he can dry his things out. Shouldn't take too long today."

Two hours later Laker was dry on the outside but like the others very wet inside. In fact only Moran who had done more than his share of time on the gun was the remotest bit sober. Even Reid was talking as much rubbish as the rest until fate mercifully took a hand and he was violently sick over the side of the boat, which caused a chain reaction and two of the AEs followed suit.

As a result, Baron was persuaded that perhaps they should head back toward Limbang, so waking Mackay who was in a drunken slumber and ordering Moran to help him below, they made ready to sail. There was no question of the AEs paddling alongside in their state so they remained sprawled along the decks while the others feigned normality as best they could.

After an hour's sailing, during which time Baron narrowly avoided hitting both banks in between driving Mackay and Moran crazy by continually changing his mind on the speed indicator on the bridge, depending on how he felt at the time. 'I'll get that bloody porridge yaffling, caber-tossing Scots bugger going.' He (Baron) decided that they were a bit ahead of schedule and better lay up for a while before getting back to base.

"OK my ansomes, we'll take a break here for a while and get a bit sobered up. Don't want the CO thinking we've been loafing all day, do we?" he grinned.

So for an hour or so they dozed, were sick overboard or related tales of their adventures all over the Far East during this commission. A highlight of their tour of duty was recalled by Lewis.

"When we were in Aussie" he started, immediately catching the interest of the more junior members who hoped that they too, might soon visit Australia during their commission.

"What's it like there then, Lewy?"

"The women are OK but the blokes are a shower of loud mouthed berks who think they know how to drink. They all piss up on little glasses of ale called schooners or midis; they drink about a dozen of these which only amounts to about four or five pints, and they're as pissed as arseoles. We drank that lot under the table regularly, no sweat. they swear like fuck too." he added as an afterthought.

"Christ, hark who's talking."

"Yeah, fair enough, but not in front of women.."

"Those sods do. We were in a really smart bar in Perth one night, d'you remember Scouse? When in walked these two scruffy as fuck buggers. They had no shoes on and stank to high heaven, Anyway, they called over this dolly bird behind the bar and said 'Give us two cans of fuckin' piss Sheila' just like that. We couldn't believe it and might have given them a piece of our minds if the bird had minded. But she never even batted an eyelid."

"That's right. Turned out they'd been Roo shooting out in the bush for a month; You know, kangaroos."

"Remember that day we were on the flight deck on Bulwark when that bootneck from the rifle company turned up in that taxi?" said Lee

"Yeah. He was a pissed as a fart and all over the place. He got out the cab and legged it for the gangway. Obviously got no cash, we thought, but the thing was that he'd spewed his ring up in the back of the taxi and the driver was chasing him up the gangway to make him clean it up."

"He would've got away, too if the Duty Pig hadn't been at the top of the plank and caught him."

"Right. The cabbie told the pig what it was all about and demanded that he do something about his cab getting cleaned up. So the pig tells this marine to go down below to get some cleaning gear and report back to him."

"There was quite a commotion so by this time half the ships company was topside watching this little lot."

"Yeah, anyway the marine finally staggers back with a bucket of water and a mop and promptly falls arse over tit on the water he'd spilt soaking the duty pig in the process. So he gets another bollicking and is sent down below again for another bucket of water which he eventually manages - just. Somehow he made it to the bottom of the gangway and across the jetty to the taxi. Then he opened the back door, slung the whole bucketful , slams the door again and staggered once again up the gangway, saluting the duty pig and saying 'number one car clean and ready for your inspection sir'. The whole fuckin' ship curled up laughing and the pig and the cab driver went fuckin' bananas. Eventually some young matelot got detailed to clean the car out and the marine got stoppage of leave for the rest of our stay in Aussie."

"Yeah. Actually we had a bloody good time in Aussie after the exercises. Mind you, I've never been so bloody hot in my life as it was in the bush there. We flew off Bulwark which for once had the air conditioning working, into the bush and it was 130 degrees Fahrenheit."

"And we were man-packing the guns, too. We came across a stretch of pure white sand exactly 1000 metres long and the bloody reflection of the sun made it like an oven to walk over. Blokes was dropping like flies. Shit, that was hot. Talking of flies, that's the place for them. Bastards are so dry there that they try to drink the liquid from your eyes and even with a camouflage net over your face they still get in."

"Dunno how those blokes can stay out there for a month at a time chasing bloody kangaroos. I think they got about ten quid a pelt if I remember rightly. Then they just piss it all up for a week and go back for more. Crazy?"

"Speaking of women, which we wasn't" said Lee "I got fixed up with a cracking bit of stuff there. Would you believe Daddy was the Managing Director of the only brewery in Perth, Swan Lager? He even offered me a top job there if I felt like jumping ship."

"So why didn't you?"

"Devoted to the Royal Corps ain't I?"

"Right Ho my ansomes, let's get cracking" ordered Baron taking an almighty swig of Brandy Wine from a bottle which he then passed on to Mackay who gratefully accepted it claiming it was just sufficient to keep him going until he got back to the engine room.

"No more cans overboard now my sons. They'll think the fuckin' NAAFI sunk or something if any more cans float past. Hope to Christ no bugger's waiting for us or keeping an eye on the river too closely."

"Never actually knew what NAAFI stood for; what does it mean Sarge? asked Bray one of the younger AEs on board.

"What does NAAFI stand for my ansomes?" bellowed Baron to his machine gunners.

"No Ambition And Fuck-All Interest" they yelled to a man.

"OK my son?"

"Thanks Sarge, but I don't really believe that." the lad replied.

"Gawd 'elp us" cried Baron. "What the hell are they dishing out of the Depot Deal these days?"

"One born every minute Sarge......."

"Never mind, eh, let's get going. Hold on to your hollihocks my lovelies. 'Ere, what's up with the boat; bloody slow all of a sudden ain't it?"

"Try pulling the fucking anchor up Sergeant" called Lewis beaming all over his face.

"Damn fine suggestion my son. All together now, heave!"

"Like fuckin' Fred Carno's army, this lot, eh Scouse?"

"Lewy, my old buddy, how could it possibly be anything else or anything better with Baron up front?"

"True."

"OK lads, get smartened up a bit, we're almost there now just a couple of bends to go now. Steady as she goes number one." he grinned to himself.

Minutes later the boat nosed its way around the final bend before the landing stage at Limbang, where four figures could be clearly seen waiting on the jetty.

"Shit. Looks like a welcoming committee. Ain't that the CO and the bloody Adjutant on the end of the pier Lewy?"

"Yeah. And the fuckin' Padre. And Robbo."

"That's all we need. Quick, get on the gun and tell Reid to get the drunken buggers down below out of the way. You'd better be the first one then, hadn't you?" he grinned.

"That's enough of your bloody lip. Anyway, I'm fine. Never felt better" beamed the profusely red faced Sergeant, humming away to himself.

"Well keep the bloody boat straight then or we'll hit the bank."

"Panic not my son. Your leader leadeth."

"I say, sir, isn't that Sergeant Knight's machine gunners on that boat coming into the jetty?" asked the Adjutant, a tall rangy man with an excessively large nose, who was well liked in the unit amongst the other ranks for his almost total incompetence as an individual, yet who would instantaneously and without hesitation agree with the slightest whim of the Commanding Officer." I think you're actually right for once, Ashwood.

"Am I really, sir? Good show.

"Where have they been?" ventured the Padre.

"Up river to a couple of kampongs, looking for arms caches, sir." replied Robson.

"Aah, brave souls" sighed the Padre. "Praise be to the Lord for their safe return."

"I say, sir, isn't the boat going rather quickly to be landing at the jetty?"

"Don't be silly Ashwood. They know what they're doing, don't they Lieutenant Robson?"

"Fine experienced men those sir. Capable of handling any craft on these waters."

"There you are Ashwood. I told you so."

"Of course, sir. How silly of me."

"Yes."

"Slow down a bit Sarge. We'll ram the buggers at this rate of knots."

"Don't panic. I'm just about to throw her into reverse. Hope Jock's on the ball down below?"

"Er, well, Jock's not exactly down below Sarge. Well, he is, but he's not really there as it were."

"What are you talking about?"

"Well." continued Laker "he's fast asleep. Snoring like a good'un."

"What? Who the bloody hell's down there then?"

"Scouse at the moment . And he's not exactly in the best of health right now, if you know what I mean."

"But he hasn't got a bloody clue. Shit. Get down there and try and get this thing slowed down, or in reverse or something, quick." shouted Baron.

"Right, Sarge."

"Are you sure Sergeant Knight knows how to handle that craft?" asked the Commanding Officer of Robson.

"Oh yes, sir" 'he damned well better' thought the Lieutenant.

"Look, he's waving to us. Hello, hello." Ashwood called as he waved back.

"Don't make a damned exhibition of yourself Ashwood. This is a theatre of war, not Battersea funfair." growled the Commanding Officer.

"Yessir. I mean no sir. Terribly sorry sir. Won't happen again sir."

"Does seem to be moving at quite a pace, though" commented the Padre.

"I knew bloody Ashwood would wave back." laughed Baron.

"He's a right doughnut."

"I think we're going to overshoot" said Lewis who had joined Baron on the bridge.

"I think we'll have to. Scouse hasn't slowed us down enough to stop so I'll have to do a sort of 'march past' at sea, then we'll swing round and come in again from the other end."

"Look out, Sarge, you're going to hit the jetty."

"Nah. I'll just swerve past it and put the shits up Ashwood. Saluting the CO at the same time, of course" he grinned.

"Don't be an arseole. You can't judge it that closely." Shouted

Lewis.

"Watch my tracer, squad."

"Oughtn't we to take evasive action, sir? I'm almost sure he's going to hit us" cried Ashwood taking a step backwards.

"Stand still Ashwood, the bows are turning away from us now. He must be going round again."

"Yessir. But the after end of the boat is sure to smack into the jetty, sir, I think."

"My God, I think he's right. Sorry Padre." exclaimed the CO.

"Left 'and down a bit. Steady as she goes. Hard to Port. Oh shit!"

With a resounding thud, the craft's rear end smacked into the jetty. One, then two of the stanchions supporting it collapsed, throwing all four officers completely off balance and onto their backs. Somehow the Commanding Officer and Robson managed to scramble back to the safety of the bank, but the unfortunate Ashwood and the Padre slid unceremoniously off the end of the jetty and into the river.

"Help!"

"Bloody 'ell Baron, now we're in the shit. That's the fuckin' Padre and bloody Ashwood in the oggin."

"No doubt the good Lord will save the Padre, but Ashwood will have to look after himself. Don't suppose I'll get any promotion now, will I?" he grinned. "Bloody funny though wasn't it?"

Did you see Ashwood's face?"

"Never mind bloody Ashwood. What are you going to say to Robson and the CO?"

"Dunno. I'll think of something. Let's get this thing back and tied up. We'll have to glide into the bank. there's nowhere else to stick it."

"Get alongside the other boat and lash them together" suggested Reid which Baron readily agreed to.

Jock Mackay having awakened about the time of impact, and though not quite in full command of his senses was very definitely in command of the engine room, so Baron had at least some assistance in easing the boat alongside the other which remained secured to the remnants of the jetty.

However, on swerving to miss some jutting pieces of timber that once were part of it Baron contrived to slice into the bow of the remaining craft, which fortunately was in only three feet of water as a large crack appeared on its water line.

More concerned with the saturated state of the Padre, and to a lesser extent Ashwood, those on the bank failed to observe Baron's slight mis-calculation, the noise of the engine covering the sound of the crack.

"Terribly sorry, sirs" said Baron on alighting from the boat.

"Slight error in judgement" smiling his most sympathetic smile to all.

"What the hell do you think that is? A damn dodgem at Billy Manning's Fairground?" stormed Robson.

"I think the rudder got caught in some thick reeds as well, sir....." started Baron.

"Don't give me that crap, Sergeant. Report to my quarters immediately."

"No, No, Lieutenant Robson. It's quite alright" spluttered the Padre. "Your men must be under considerable pressure, and they're not sailors after all."

"But sir........"

"I insist no further action be taken" said the Padre.

"They have, by the look of them had a most strenuous days' patrol and must be very, very tired now, so a minor error is understandable in the circumstances."

"If you insist, sir."

"Get your men to their billet Sergeant. You have no guard or patrol duty tonight so be ready for an early start in the morning. Do I make myself quite clear?"

"Positively, sir. Thank you, Padre."

"A pleasure, my son. God bless you."

"You're a lucky sod, Baron" breathed Mackay.

"Suppose you could say that. But there again, the devil looks after his own, eh?" smiled Baron.

"Him and bloody Derry. I can't stand that snivelling little pratt either. Gets right up my throat. But I'll have the bastard before we leave this place, that's for sure."

"Where's the little shit now, anyway?"

"All the mortars are down at the fish market. Best place for them. Half that lot get on my tit. Not like the old lot we had out here when we joined 42, eh?"

"Nah. There were a few characters then. Remember old Jim Curser? That night he got pissed out of his skull up the NAAFI and someone bet him he wouldn't eat a turd sarnie and drink a pint of piss? Fastest hundred bucks he ever made, he reckoned afterwards. Mind you, he spewed for two days after."

"Yeah, and Snowy White. He was a bloody player OK. Got high on the grass one day and thought he was a bleedin' flag of all things; went over to the flag pole on the Main Parade, tied one end of the rope around his throat and tried to pull himself up to the top of the mast. Fuckin' near hung himself. Good job the patrol came by or he would have done."

"Pass that bloody brandy over, Scouse."

"Not bad this stuff; especially as Levine's paying for it."

"I'd like to stick my rifle right up Levine's arse and pull the trigger. Little bastard. Got me three days inside for pissing over his car once." said Lee, swigging hard at a bottle.

"Remember that time we was in Aden on that stupid exercise with the bloody Paras?"

"Yeah. The arseole of the bloody world is Aden. What a fuckin' dump. I hate those bastards anyway. Dirty sods."

"But do you remember when old Buck Taylor was on watch on the gun in the middle of the night? He was so cold, well, you know how cold it gets in the desert at night, enough to freeze 'em off. So Buck decides to wrap himself up in a camouflage net and have a crafty burn to keep warm. Trouble was, he was so knackered he fell asleep halfway through it. Next minute , the whole bloody lot's on fire."

"The Lord said, let there be light, and there was light. And you could see for fuckin' miles."

"Yeah, but they only just dragged him out in time. The CO went fucking spare. We'd spent the best part of four hours creeping up to that position in the dark ready for a damn attack on the bloody cherry berets and here it was like bloody Blackpool."

"All old Buck said he remembered was some bugger pissing on

him."

"Pass the bottle."

"Y 'know, the more I think about that bleeding Derry, the more I feel like havin' him."

"Leave it out. He' s not worth it, Lewy."

"Balls. I'm going for a little stroll. Where's my bloody SMG?"

"Don't be bloody daft, there's a curfew on. You'll get shot yourself. There's patrols and ambushes all over the place."

"I don't give a monkeys. I'm off. See yuh."

"Fuck you then, stupid bastard." Slipping out the door so as not to waken the rest of the platoon who were all asleep in the next room, Lewis headed down the main road towards the fish market, staggering from side to side and on one occasion falling flat on his face in a ditch. As he approached the fish market, he started to sing and this saved his life for, on hearing the drunken strains of 'Strangers in the Night' the alert sentries had ceased from firing only because of the fact that the song was sung in English. The next thing Lewis knew was a hand grabbing him around the throat and the very definite feel of a rifle in his back, as he was pushed into the safety of a position behind a wall where the other members of the ambush he had stumbled into waited.

"Where's bleedin' Derry asked Lewis."

"I'm going to blow his bloody head off."

"I'll give you two minutes to get sober or I'll personally blow your fucking brains out, if you've got any which I doubt after this, you stupid bastard. How the hell you got this far I don't know, but now I've got to send out two blokes to get you back in one piece, though it'd serve you right if I just push you out and let you find your own way back. You two. Know the password OK?"

"Yeah."

"Try and pull a stunt like that again Lewis and I'll pull the trigger first and ask questions afterwards. Understand?"

"OK. I'm sorry. Won't happen again. Thanks, Lads. The booze, y'know."

"Go on piss off before I change my mind and lock you up and throw the fucking key away." Successfully negotiating their way back to the MMGs office with only one encounter with a friendly patrol, Lewis collapsed on his sleeping-bag and was asleep in seconds.

After a short patrol the next day, they prepared themselves for their night duty which was to replace the mortars in the fish market for the night. No sooner had they settled down for an early meal than the door burst open and one of the AEs came in.

"Don't you knock when entering people's private residences?" asked Lee.

"Very funny. But Sergeant, you'd better get down to the jetty. That boat you hit is slowly sinking and there's possibly some stores on it."

"Christ," said Mackay "those two bloody great batteries are down below in the hold. If the water level reaches the top of them they'll bloody well explode and blow half of bloody Limbang sky high."

"Stay here, Laker. The rest follow me. Hurry up."

Once on board they quickly located the hold the batteries were in and Baron and Mackay assessed the situation. Shining their torches down into the black abyss below them they could see that the water level had now risen so that it was barely inches from the top of the batteries.

The hold itself was only about six feet square and in this confined space stood the batteries and the ladder leading down into it.

"I'll have to get down there on the double. I'll need a hand to lift them out though" said Baron.

"Come on Lewy, shake a leg, my son."

"Bloody 'ell. Why do I get all the nice jobs?"

"Cos you're my favourite" grinned Baron.

"I love you, too. No shit you bastard." Baron eased his large frame down into the hold and as slowly as possible trying as hard as possible not to cause a ripple, edged his way to the far side of the box containing the batteries. Meanwhile Mackay and Lee tried to get as much light as they could down on him. Knee deep in water he then called Lewis down. "For Chrissake don't make a wave my son or we'll be on angel cake for the rest of our lives."

"That's all I need; you cracking bloody jokes while I'm risking life and limb. Shine that light over here Jock. Can't see a fuckin' thing."

Cautiously Lewis made his way towards and opposite Baron. There was hardly any room for them to move now and their own bodies constantly blocked out the light as hard as Mackay and Lee tried.

The batteries were encased in a large wooden crate but so tightly were they fitted into it that there was hardly space for their fingers to get around the batteries. Bent over double, they gradually managed to get a grip on one battery and, facing each other, slowly started to ease it out of the crate.

Each battery weighed over thirty pounds so it was with no mean effort that the two strained to get the first battery out. Sweat was now pouring from them as they struggled in the shadowy light. Half straightening up with the battery now held firmly between them, Lewis looked to Baron for an inkling of their next move and in the beam of the torchlight, caught Baron's gaze. Baron was grinning from ear to ear.

"What the bloody hell are you grinning at?"

"I was just thinking of a time I got caught in something similar to this in Palestine. Bloody funny bugger I was with then ,too."

"Oh, bloody charming."

"Never thought I'd spend my Xmas holidays in the bottom of a boat in the dark with another marine, holding up a battery. Funny ain't it?"

"Definitely. Please don't start me off laughing just now Baron or I'll just as likely drop this bugger!"

"What the bloody hell's up with you two?" called Mackay. For Chrissake git a grip on yourselves. Drop that bleeding battery and we'll all go up. And in case you've forgotten, there's another bugger in the box and the water is still rising. So move it."

"Yeah. C'mon Baron. Joke over."

"Good to have a laugh at Xmas though ain't it?"

Straining their every muscle the two, with the aid of the willing hands above, managed to get the first battery up the steep ladder to safety. The second proved a much easier task and with great relief Mackay hauled it onto the deck above.

"You two sods want hanging from" he said as at last Baron and Lewis joined the others.

"Fancy standing down a black hold, in two feet of water with a potential bomb in your hands and giggling like a couple of school kids."

"I really thought we'd shit it for a minute there. My guts were killing me trying to hold that bloody thing and laughing at this bugger as well."

"All good fun" laughed Baron. "Let's get our heads down then, eh?"

"I need a bloody drink first. I do take it that this little episode excludes me from guard duty tonight?"

"Not an ice cube in hells chance I'm afraid my old son. We're all on tonight. Serves you right. Never volunteer for sod all my ansom." grinned Baron.

"Where the bloody hell's Batu Apoi?" asked Laker.

"Up river somewhere, towards Brunei. We're going there with the Mortars and the AEs, so we'll be away from the rest of the unit. Should be OK. Not so many buggers trying to take charge and keep an eye on us."

"Only Robbo."

"He's no problem."

"Don't be too sure. You won't have the Padre to look after you now."

"Trust in your leader my sons. I've looked after you so far, haven't I?" grinned Baron.

Batu Apoi

Batu Apoi proved to be nothing but a large timber built school on the banks of the river. Surrounded by jungle apart from a clearing to the front and rear, the building itself was comprised of four large classrooms at ground level and five smaller rooms on the first floor which soon became Robsons sleeping quarters and the Operations room and the store rooms. The Machine Gunners, Mortars and Assault Engineers bedded down on the lower level, looking out onto the small expanse of neatly trimmed grass leading to the jetty, at the bottom of which were the six dugouts the troops had used to reach their location. Baron and the MMGs had been rather sad to leave their larger craft at Limbang but had, through such devious methods as storing rows of bottles in the machine gun boxes, managed to bring with them a good percentage of their goodies. Lee and Lewis, however, felt this was a move in the right direction towards getting them back to Brunei and more importantly, back to Singapore and then England.

A dozen steps led from the top of the jetty down to the dugouts and, quite expectedly, Laker had parted company with them at one stage and decided he'd prefer a swim, much to the mirth of his comrades and the annoyance of Robson who resigned himself to the fact that he might as well accept the inevitable.

"If I'd wanted to be a fuckin' matelot I'd have joined the bloody Navy" was Laker's only recourse.

"No chance of your putting in for a transfer then, I assume." cracked Robson expecting at least a ripple of laughter which, as usual did not materialise.

"Correct, sir. No Chance. Sorry to spoil your dreams. Sir."

Intelligence reports indicated that the area was being used for the smuggling and storing of arms and ammunition and the duties the Company were assigned were to send out as many patrols and ambushes as possible to try and stop the flow of arms to rebel strongholds further north. After an O Group, Baron returned with details of a patrol the Machine Gunners alone were to go on the next day to a large village ten miles away where they were to observe and report on the size of the populace, any unusual happenings in the area and the numbers of people entering and leaving the village.

"Ten bleedin' miles!" Shave off. That's twenty there and back. We'll be too bloody knackered to fight any bugger after tracking through that amount of ulu." cried Moran.

"Don't panic, squad. There's tracks nearly all the way there apparently so it won't be so bad. Anyway. I have a little scheme filtering through already" Baron chuckled.

"Christ, now what's he up to?"

"Have faith my sons. We set off at first light, so tonight get a manpack each organised and your gear ready." he smiled.

"Manpacks? Surely to Christ we're not manpacking the bloody guns twenty miles through the bloody ulu are we?" said Lewis.

"Who said anything about guns? Just get a manpack each and trust your leader my ansomes."

"Talking of choices, who's for a little game then? Or would you prefer a verse or two from Rudyard?"

"Decisions, decisions. Think I'll just piss off and get me bloody head down if we're yomping all that bloody way tomorrow" said Laker. "I could murder a bleeding pint right now, too."

"You never know when the Good Lord will provide my sons. Just be patient" grinned Baron, winking.

The patrol left the school at dawn the following morning through the steamy mist which always rises through the jungle when there is a river or water around. Probing through the thick undergrowth they soon became very wet and uncomfortable as the moisture dropped from the trees along with an unusually numerous amount of leeches which festooned the foliage. Stops were regular with the exception of one enforced when Luther, as lead scout, pulled a large branch away from him only find a huge black and yellow furry spider in a web only inches from his face. His sharp yell had the reminder diving for cover until he informed them that there was no enemy at hand but his experience had made him fill his trousers so a stop for him to clean himself up with de-leeched leaves was necessary. He was then sent to the back of the patrol as tail end Charlie.

Soon afterwards they hit a track which they followed for nearly three miles until Baron and Mackay concluded that it must lead directly into the village they sought which proved to be the case. Estimating that they were now barely half a mile from the village, Baron pulled the patrol off the track and back into the jungle, while still following its course. The terrain now was more sparsely populated with jungle so their progress was slower and more cautious as they approached the village. Also the ground now climbed to a considerable height and it was not long before they heard the sounds associated with a village. Signalling to the others to take defensive cover behind him , Baron led Mackay to a position from which they were able to view the proceedings ahead and below them.

"Looks normal enough, eh?"

"Yeah. Bigger than I thought it would be Jock. Must be a dozen or more bashers there. Gimme the binos."

"See anything startling?"

"Found what I was looking for. I think it's OK to go and have a little looksee. What do you reckon?"

"Yeah. Better be careful though. Looks a bit too quiet and peaceful to me."

"OK. You take Laker, Moran and Luther with you and take the right side of the village. Me, Lee and Lewis will take the left. Let's get back to the others."

"Right. Hang about Sarge. What did you mean just now when you said you'd found what you were looking for?"

"You'll see, my son" grinned Baron.

"The plot thickens, eh?" Scrambling back to the others Baron relayed his orders. "Keep your eyes open, lads. Try not to look aggressive, though how the hell you're going to do that Laker beats me" he laughed.

"Laugh a minute ain't he?" replied Laker.

"And for Chrissake don't fire at any bastard unless you have to. Just take a casual look around the bashers on your side of the village. Two inside, one out, OK be nice and friendly, like. Show the flag and all that crap, alright? Let's go then. Spread out my sons." Back out onto the track, the patrol moved into the village each group taking their respective side. The villagers appeared not only curious but pleased to see them and they smiled and chatted away and waved at the troops as they advanced along the road which bi-sected the kampong. Even when the marines entered the shacks they were shown no hostility in fact, as was quite common in Borneo many of the bashers had large photographs and paintings of the British Royal Family displayed on the walls.

Mackay's men having reached the end of the village, waited and watched as Baron's group steadily advanced towards them until they too reached the last and biggest basher which dominated the whole kampong.

"Hold on here you two while I have a quick scout in here" said Baron indicating the two marines to wait outside the basher.

Baron was not disappointed in his theory that the largest basher in the kampong would be the one most likely to contain supplies of some description.

"Over here, lads" he called on returning to the entrance. "This is the one we've been looking for" he grinned.

"What's up Sarge? Is it an arms cache?" asked Luther.

"Arms cache my arse. This is where they keep the goodies. What do you think we've carried these bloody manpacks all this way for? Bloody show?"

"Sorry, O great white leader, I should've known better" Luther mimicked.

"I should fucking cocoa. Right, Jock, spread the others around in some sort of defensive postion. Lee and Lewis come with me. Going to do a spot of shopping, chaps. Won't be a mo."

"Now he thinks he's back in bleedin' Tesco's."

Leading them back into the shack Baron proudly pointed to the object of his pleasure. Rows and rows of canned food, fresh vegetables and , most importantly several crates of beer and a fine display of spirits spread along two walls.

"OK my ansomes, now do you see the reasoning behind the manpacks?"

"Fuck me" exclaimed Lewis. "How the hell do they get all this stuff out here in the middle of nowhere?"

"Along the rivers and then they hump it through the ulu.

"But how do they pay for it?" asked Lewis.

"Two ways, I reckon. They trade their fruits from the jungle and don't know if you noticed those patches of stuff growing on that sort of allotment back there, but I reckon they're growing and flogging their own brand of grass. Probably the base from which half the drugs in the Far Flung come. Possible?"

"Could be. Anyway who gives a fuck? Let's get stuck into this little lot."

"Hang about. We haven't come here for a piss up. We'll load up and get it all back to camp before we start on it."

"Not even just one smallie drink Sarge?" begged Lee.

"Negative. Get the others in here, or better still, form a chain and pass it out so they can load the packs."

The abundant supplies in the store were pillaged with little or no concern for the protesting and now not so friendly owner who was finally subdued with an impressive chitty produced and signed by Sergeant Knight.

"Pity we've got to fuck off just yet Lewy. There's a couple of fair looking pieces of fanny around. Look at that thing in the green over there" said Lee pointing to a particularly well endowed young girl.

"Yeah, but have you seen the teeth on it? Black as arseoles. Must chew those bloody beetle nuts. Get those round yer fuckin' chopper and it'll drop off in a fortnight."

"What a way to go, though."

"C'mon, we're on the move again. Good old Baron. Does it every time eh? Don't quite know how we're going to get this lot into camp without Robbo and the others seeing it. do you?"

"Probably have to share a bit out to keep the peace."

"Baron'll think of something. He always does."Baron had indeed thought of something. He ensured that the patrol returned to their base just as darkness was descending on the place. With very little difficulty a couple of manpacks which carried the more choice items, such as brandy and tins of prawns, were discreetly hidden in the undergrowth close by until they could be retrieved in complete privacy. The remainder were carefully stowed away in the machine gun boxes and amongst empty ammunition liners.

The next two days at the camp were spent in a rather idyllic manner. On the expanse of grass in front of the school a volleyball court was rigged and a football pitch marked out. There ensued some rough battles between the platoons with several minor injuries resulting including a black eye for Robson when he was persuaded to keep goal for the Mortars and got in the way of a blockbuster from Lee. Night times were spent on patrols or ambushes and for the Machine Gunners in their off duty moments quietly sipping the product of their march, whilst patiently listening to renderings of Baron's past interspersed with the inevitable Rudyard.

Food for the company as a whole was at a premium but once again Baron came to the rescue with the idea of fishing for their food from the river. His methods had not quite met with his commander's approval, but Robson had only discovered Baron's way of fishing by chance on returning from a trip up river to an O Group one morning earlier than expected. The sound of explosions had forced Robson to beach his dugout half a mile short of the camp and hack his way, with his escort and signaller, through thick jungle back to base, thinking that it was under attack, only to find the intrepid Baron casually tossing hand grenades into the river trying to kill and stun sufficient fish to be gathered for food.

"That's my promotion up the shit again." bemoaned Baron.

"Bloody Robbo damn soon ate the bloody fish though, didn't he?"

"Two faced bastard."

"Sit down Sergeant Knight."

"Yessir."

"I have something very important to tell you."

"Something wrong with the fish, sir?"

"No it was rather nice actul.........Shut up Sergeant and listen to me!"

"Yessir."

"This morning's O Group provided some interesting Intelligence reports on a particular basher just a couple of miles from our location where it would appear that two rebels are apparently running arms by

90

night and holing up by day. Now, we have been ordered to investigate and I have evolved a plan which you and your platoon are to execute this very evening. Is that clear so far, Sergeant?"

"As a bell, sir. As a bell."

"Good. Right then. I want three dugouts with two of your men in each, to leave this location at midnight tonight. You will paddle silently and I emphasise silently, up river to this location and once there you will disembark, hide your dugouts somewhere along the bank of the river and make your way to the basher. Once there, you will place yourself and your men under the basher and wait until these two creatures return to it which should be shortly before dawn. Do you understand?

"Yessir. No problem."

"So far so good. When they do eventually return you will arrest them and search the basher for anything that could be of the slightest interest to Intelligence or us. And by us I mean Headquarters, Sergeant, not the Machine Gun Platoon. Do I make myself quite clear?"

"Clear as a bell, sir."

"I hope so Sergeant."

"You can rely on the MMGs, sir."

"And ensure that your men are completely sober, Sergeant. Silence is vital to the success of this mission, and the success of this mission is vital." said Robson, rather cleverly, he thought.

"That's all very clear, sir."

"I shall be at the jetty to see your leave Sergeant. Do not be late."

"Very good sir."

"Gather round your leader my sons. Time for a pow-wow from the big white chief." Said Baron grinning.

"Thinks he's a bloody red Indian now."

"Right lads, tonight we're going on a little pleasure cruise. Well, not exactly tonight, more of your early hours touch. Make a nice change from lying around here in the sun all day, eh?"

"Oh Christ, not another Mission Impossible, please. After that last effort with the AEs at Limbang, my nerves won't stand anymore."

"No this is different."

"It's always bloody is 'til we get at it."

"Now listen. Joke over for now. We've been honoured with an important patrol. We're going to paddle up stream tonight, or tomorrow morning rather in the dugouts, find some basher and wait under it until a couple of rebels come back to it at first light after a night running arms around the countryside. Then we'll capture them and bring them and any other interesting gear we can find back here to be examined by Robbo. OK? Simple, no problems."

"Sounds easy enough. But then it always does 'till us lot get at it."

"Ever the optimist........"

"Right, now let's get the dugouts ready before the sun goes down, then we can have a little kip. Make sure your gear is on the ball though before you all start piling up the zeds. Just SMGs and two magazines each. Any questions?"

"I thought the bloody Cockleshell Heroes all died in the last war?"

"Most of them did. But we are the new breed."

"You didn't volunteer us for this little lot by any chance did you?" asked Lee.

"You should know better than that Scouser. Never volunteer my sons. I learnt that the first day I was in the Royal Corps. Fell in on parade and the Drill Sergeant asked for a volunteer who had musical tendencies. Being a bit of a honky tonk piano man I thought I'd get in his good books at an early stage and stuck me hand up. The bugger got me and two others to go to his house first thing on a Sunday morning and shift his bleedin' piano up three flights of stairs. Never volunteered for fuck all else since."

"We all learn the hard way I suppose." said Laker." Like me and those bloody bridges I keep falling off."

"Trouble is , you still haven't learned how to get across the buggers."

"Yeah, but I'm getting better ain't I?"

"Without a doubt, my son" called Baron while he made a more comfortable space for his sleeping bag on the floor. "Who's got the cork for blacking out? Might as well get organised now, eh? Does anybody feel like a verse or two before we get our heads down?" And not waiting fror a reply he continued "Soldier and Sailor Too................."

"C'mon my sons. Rise and shine. Hands off cocks on socks. Let's get with it. Time to go on our world cruise."

"Shit. I was just about to give Marilyn Monroe the thrill of a lifetime."

"You couldn't give bloody No Nose a thrill."

"Bollicks."

"While you're getting yourselves organised lads, I'll put you in the picture. The corks are over there by the way. Now, I'll be in the first canoe with Jock and Ginge, cos it's a big one, eh?" Lewy and Scouser will be in the next one and Moran and Lakes in the third. Any questions?"

"Who paddles? The front man or the back?"

"The rear man will paddle."

"You're in the back Scouse."

"Cheers, hoppo."

"Now it's vital that we don't give ourselves away, so there'll be no talking from the moment we leave here 'til we get back. Not a bloody sound, OK? No-one is to fire at any time unless absolutely necessary. Understood? When we reach the basher I'll put each man in position. Again, not a sound from anyone. No bastard will come within a hundred miles if we make the slightest noise and we'll have spent the night under a bleeding basher for nothing when we could've been tucked up in our little pits getting some shuteye. OK, now you've got five minutes for a fag and a piss while I check each one of you to make sure you don't rattle. Though I'll have to take into account Lake's brains won't I?" laughed Baron.

"Go on take the piss. I'm getting used to it by now."

"Aaah. Everybody go aah." Mimicked Baron.

"C'mon Lewy, you're first. Jump up and down for Sarge, there's a good boy."

"PTI's on your heads bounce. UP, up, up and steady."

"One thing Sarge, how the bloody hell are we supposed to keep together out there in the pitch dark?" asked Lindon smearing his face with burnt cork."

"Just keep your ears open and listen for the sound of the paddles in the water from the boat ahead of you. Ears open, gobs shut. Any last minute questions then?"

"Can't we have a quick whet before we fuck off Sarge?" asked Lee.

"No chance. Bloody Robbo will be on the jetty to see us piss off and if we go out there smelling like a bloody brewery he'll go bananas and I'll never get promoted, will I?" he grinned.

Reaching the jetty they found Robson waiting for them with the two sentries on duty. Without a word Baron signalled his men to follow him down the steps of the jetty to the boats waiting below.

In the still, humid night, the final segment of the moon provided a minimum of light. The only sounds were those of the multitude of insects that abounded around the river and the jungle and the gentle lapping of the water against the pillars of the jetty.

The three dugouts were secured alongside each other so that to reach their craft Baron, Mackay and Linden had to climb over the other two. In comparative silence they successfully made it and cast off into a position ten yards from the jetty to await the others.

Moran then led Laker into the second boat. Feeling his way up front Moran held onto the rope securing the craft ready to slip the noose. As he did so he felt the boat rock slightly as Laker climbed aboard and just managed to maintain his balance as he released the rope. However, turning round he realised that Laker had not quite finished boarding, for the unfortunate marine was at that moment doing a wonderful attempt at the splits with one foot on one canoe and the other on the remaining craft still tied to the jetty. And the distance between them grew greater by the second. He could neither lever himself forward or back and with his Sub Machine Gun in one hand, his other grabbed desperately for something to cling to. There was nothing to cling to. With a resounding splash and a plaintive cry of 'fuck me' Laker plunged into the dark waters.

"What's happened?" hissed Robson from the top of the jetty.

"Sergeant Knight, what's going on?"

By now, Baron's canoe had drifted slowly down river a short distance and Macky and Lindon were ordered to pull into the jetty again. On arriving there they were now positioned behind Robson on the opposite side to the remaining canoes. While Mackay held the craft steady, Baron climbed up the structure and finally reached up and clung to the top of the jetty at the same time inadvertently tapping the unsuspecting officer on the leg.

"I think somebody's fallen in sir. Probably Laker again." Taken completely by surprise at having his leg grabbed from behind by someone he thought to be in the opposite direction, Robson gave a start, whirled round and in the process inadvertently trod on the hapless Sergeant's hands. Letting out an almighty yell, Baron fell back down into the boat which had it not been for both Mackay and Linden keeping a firm grip on the stanchions, would also have capsized.

"Sergeant Knight, this is a bloody farce; get that man out of the water and get this patrol moving at once." hissed Robson angrily.

"Yessir."

Laker had now been dragged into their canoe by Moran, swearing and cursing the entire concept of Royal Marines, canoes, water and why the bloody hell hadn't he stayed in that nice warm factory in dear old Wolverhampton.

"And keep all this noise down" Robson whispered venomously through the darkness

"Bit bloody late for that. There's less noise when a bleedin' VC 10 takes off."

"Shut up that man."

"Bloody Fred Carno's army this is."

"The next man who utters a word will be on a charge." And Robson stormed off in disgust, leaving orders that the sentries were to report to him when 'this bloody abortion finally gets mobile'.

"Scouse, I think I've pissed myself laughing" said Lewis.

"Lakes has, that's for sure."

Gathering some semblance of order, the three canoes finally managed to rendezvous in the centre of the river and after a very much tongue in cheek lecture from Baron, finally set off on their mission. The thick jungle along the river was barely perceptible except for the multitude of insect life that fluttered amongst it much of which was luminous, but that served as guide enough to keep them a safe distance from the bank.

Led by Baron they slowly progressed keeping as close to each other and the bank as possible. However, Baron had not foreseen the possibility of fallen branches languishing in the shallows and his canoe piled headlong into one thickly foliaged tree which suddenly appeared ahead. Too late, the ensuing canoes followed suit until all three were tangled up with the tree and each other.

"Fuckin' shave off."

"Ouch. Get that bleedin' paddle out of my head."

"Back off for Chrissake."

"Shhh."

"Never mind bloody Shh. Get this branch out the canoe Scouse.".

"Christ, I hope there's no bleedin' Tiger snakes on it or in the middle of this that's all we fucking need."

Tiger snakes were a problem for the marines especially when they were on water, for the snakes would often drop from an overhanging branch onto their dugouts as they passed below.

Eventually disengaging themselves from the branches of the fallen tree, Baron decided that as they were roughly only a half mile or so from their destination, they would continue on foot, so carefully and as quietly as possible they beached their craft and gathered together for Baron's whispered instructions.

"Right lads, it's only about half a mile away, so we'll follow the line of the river until we hit it. Follow me and no noise, OK?"

"How the bloody hell can I be silent" asked Laker "when I'm fucking soaked to the skin and squelching around like a bleedin' Wrens march past?"

"Don't make us laugh now Lakes, for fuck's sake. My sides still hurt from that episode at the jetty."

"It's alright for you bastards, I'm the one who's fuckin' wet."

"You got that right."

"Very funny, arseole.

"That's enough you lot, now let's move and shut up."

Groping through the thick jungle they proceeded towards their target which took them longer than expected to reach. As they finally did so there was the merest hint of dawn breaking and even though it was still dark in the jungle, the sky above slowly lightened as they lay watching the path Baron and Mackay had taken to reconnoitre the basher they were to watch. Returning, Baron placed Laker where he was, Linden and Moran at two other possible escape routes from the basher, and beckoned Mackay, Lee and Lewis to accompany him under the hut.

Built on stilts as were most of the bashers in the jungle, especially near the rivers, they found underneath it a collection of earthenware pots and dishes and tools which they settled down between to await the contact they hoped soon to make.

Suddenly, they were no longer alone for wandering into the clearing and heading straight for them was a dog, scrawny and hungry it was scratching for food as it sniffed its way towards them. These animals that ran wild among the kampongs were extremely vicious, more so when they were as hungry as this one obviously was. Sniffing its way under the basher it was suddenly aware that it was not alone and a low growl started to emerge from its throat. Had it been given the chance to bark, their cover would have been blown. But it never got the chance. Lee saw to that. The animal had concentrated its gaze on the large form of Baron and not seen Lee hiding behind a particularly large pot. Before it had time to determine its next move or even to bark at all, Lee had it by the throat and with one arm and his entire weight crushing it to the ground, calmly slit its throat with his bayonet. With blood spurting all over him, the dog whimpered and died. Lee, also covered in blood and sweating profusely, lowered the carcass to the ground and acknowledged Baron's thumbs up signal.

Now the first streaks of dawn pierced the sky and the jungle came alive. From way off along the river the dawn was heralded by the crowing of a cockerel which set a chain reaction all along the river banks as each kampong in turn replied with its own cockerel chorus until the whole length of the river seemed to become a large farmyard. Then again, they suddenly had company, but this time it was in the form of two young children who had clambered down the steps of the basher and were curiously watching them from the bottom of the steps. Two boys, unkempt, bright eyed inquisitive and not in the least afraid, they stared at first one marine and then another. A moment later they were joined by a young woman whose feet the marines trained their weapons on as they descended from the steps. Dressed in a shabby green sarong the woman was made aware of the marines presence by her offspring and hurriedly gathered them to her scooping both up in her arms.

"OK missie. We're not going to hurt you" said Baron breaking the silence and crawling out towards the woman.

"Your man in basher?" he asked

"No man" the woman replied, fear creeping into her bright eyes."

"Where is he then?"

"Gone. Man gone. Long time. Me no-one. Only babies."

"Bullshit" said Lee moving menacingly towards her, his bayonet in line with her throat.

"Leave it Scouser. We'll just have a quick shufty through the basher first. Don't want a bullet up our arseoles, do we?" grinned Baron.

"I'll keep a lookout here, Sarge, with the others" called MacKay from the other side of the basher.

"OK Jock."

"Don't mind if we check your pad, do you lady?" asked Baron starting to climb the rickety steps.

"Come on Lewy, you come with me."

"I'll wait until you're up at the top. I don't trust those bloody steps with your weight on them."

"Cheeky sod. OK, I'm up now. No-one here, anyway."

"Anything worth looking at Sarge?" said Lewis as he reached the top of the steps and peered inside.

"Come see for yourself. Bugger all, really." Inside, Lewis saw just a large bed obviously shared by the woman and her children, a few pots and bamboo mats, a picture of the Queen and a bunch of ferns scattered over the floor. "Not a lot, eh?"

"Nah. Could be some bugger kipping here though, you never know."

"Well he must've had a good night out on the piss 'cos he ain't here, is he?"

"If the truth be known, he probably heard us coming and pissed off a bit smartish."

"I reckon half the bleedin' rebel nation heard us coming. Couldn't help it."

"What's the betting Robson will go spare when we get back?"

"From what I heard at the jetty, he'll have us on fucking patrols and ambushes for the next month continuous. Bastard. Fucking funny though" laughed Lewis.

"Alright for you, I'm the one who gets the bollicking."

"Don't think you're going to get that little crown over the stripes just yet, do you?"

"No bleedin' chance." growled Baron. "Come on let's piss off. Sod all here to interest us." Climbing back down the steps, Lewis and Baron found the remainder of the patrol with the exception of Laker waiting for them.

"Come on lads, let's go. Nothing here of interest to us. Don't suppose the bint has said fuck all, Scouse?"

"Not a dicky. Maybe I should try a bit of friendly persuasion?"

"No, leave it out. Think of the kids, besides can't have those poor little sods upset, can we?"

"Bring me another smally boy; this one's split!" cried Moran

"Fuckin' Lech."

"Yeah, nice ain't it."

"Come on. There's no need to hang around here any longer. And I'm getting bleedin' starving, too."

"Me too."

"Right. Are we all gathered? Oh Christ, where's bloody Laker?"

"You put him over there somewhere, by the track, as a cut off Sarge" said Mackay.

"Better go and find him I suppose. That'll be all we need if he's been bloody snatched."

"Sent on a patrol to snatch some bugger, and get one of our own taken. Christ, that'd please bloody Robbo." said Luther.

"Wouldn't make Lakes too bloody happy, either."

"Come and look at this lads" called Moran who had wandered over to Laker's last known position.

"Fucking Sleeping Beauty."

There, snoring like a baby, his whole body steaming as the first warm rays of sunlight combined with his own body heat slowly started to dry out his clothes lay Laker.

"Why don't we just filter away and let him get on with it?"

"We can't leave Lakes. There'd be no bugger to take the piss out of."

"I expect Robbo would notice him missing anyway. Be too quiet and peaceful."

"Laker!" roared Baron as he approached Laker. "What the bloody hell do you think this is? A fucking Ban-yan?"

"Shit. What's up? Bloody hell, nobody's been this way Sarge, honest" spluttered Laker struggling to his feet.

"Half the bloody Tank Corps could have done a pussers march past and you wouldn't have known . Get your off your arse and get moving before you fry up."

"Right-o Sarge. Sorry Sarge. Where's my bloody SMG?"

Paddling back at a steady pace, the three canoes took barely half an hour to reach the jetty.

"Oh shit. Look who's waiting for us" said Lewis in the leading canoe.

"Balls. I reckon Baron's in for a right bollicking now?" said Lee.

"Too right. But it wasn't his fault there was no bugger at the basher was it?"

"If there was, they'd have heard us lot bleedin' ages before we got near the place."

"Still, it was a good laugh, though, eh?"

"Yeah, but by the way bloody Robbo's looking at us from up there laughing's the last thing on his mind."

"He's stood there like bloody Genghis Khan; look at him."

Hands on hips, legs astride Robson was an imposing, though sleight figure atop the jetty, but there was no doubting the stern expression on his face.

"Report to me in five minutes Sergeant" he stuttered, then turned on his heels and strode off towards the school.

"Here we go again........" mulled Baron.

"Shit. just as we get bloody organised, we have to piss off. How far away is whatever it's called?" asked Linden.

"Trusan. About twenty miles upriver towards Brunei. We're joining the rest of the Company there apparently, mores' the pity" be-moaned Baron.

"So we'll have even more bastards on our backs now."

"Yeah. Why don't they just leave us alone to fight the war all by ourselves?"

"Don't you mean rape and pillage?"

"Yeah, that too."

The news of their imminent departure was greeted with mixed feelings by the platoon; Lee and Lewis in particular. Whilst it would be much worse for them to be with the rest of the Company and more under the watchful eye of their superiors, it was at the same time another step neared Brunei and, they felt, repat.

Trusan

Arranged in sticks of five, the AEs, Mortars and MMGs waited for the helicopters to arrive and ferry them to their new location. The last of the machine gunners 'supplies' had been heartily consumed the night before and with the exception of Baron, all felt somewhat jaded and not looking forward to a flight.

"Whose bright idea was it to mix all the last drops of booze into one mess tin "My fuckin' head's killing me." moaned Lewis.

"I reckon you put something else in with that lot Scouse. Old Lakes is spewing his ring up again, out the back."

"Teach him to be a bloody pig, won't it? Bastard drank the last lot while I was having a slash."

"Grab your gear and somebody get Lakes. I can hear the choppers on the way" called Baron.

"How the hell are they going to get down on this small pad. I'm buggered if I know."

"Probably land up in the river, with Lewy bringing them in."Lewis had been detailed to act as marshaller for the choppers. Bringing them in on so small a pad called for an experienced hand, and Lewis had regularly been the Company's marshaller on various exercises.

Despite Lewis not feeling at his best, the choppers landed and left safely and three hours later the whole company were in Trusan.

Trusan proved to be a most picturesque little shanty town on the banks of the river which had broadened considerably and become much stronger flowing. One row of fifteen shacks faced the river across a cobbled road at the other side of which were just two buildings, a police station alongside another single storey building. The police station was manned by four Sarawak Rangers whose duties were to maintain law and order throughout the locality which included several kampongs east and west along the river, plus those scattered deep into the surrounding jungle.

Above the town on a large hill was the school building which was designated as Company Headquarters. The remaining rooms in the building were assigned to the Mortars, Assault Engineers, Headquarters staff and the Mobat crews. The Machine Gunners were despatched down to the town to share the police station with the Rangers.

Nothing could have suited them better. Or Robson.

With a gleam in his eye Baron led his men down into the town and their billet.

"Come on my ansomes. Us has been banished to the farthest corner of the Empire, I'm bloody glad to say."

"Where are we off to now then Sarge?"

"I've secured us a nice little hotel down in the town."

"You mean Robson has told us to piss off and find somewhere else as far away from him as possible to exist. If we must exist." said Mackay.

"Something like that, but have no fear my sons; your leader will look after you." Grinned Baron

"I was afraid of that."

The police station was the only building in the town that was made of concrete materials and consisted of a large back room with a kitchen and toilet attached and a front office looking over the road in which was to be found one table, one phone and two chairs and a filing cabinet. Sparse but adequate.

Baron approached the corporal in command of the four Rangers as they reached the station. "You speakie de Eegleesh?" he asked

"Better than the honourable Sergeant by the sounds of it" the corporal replied much to the amusement of all.

"Oh yeah. Got a right joker here lads. I'll soon sort this bugger out. Right ho then sunshine. I'm Sergeant Knight and this is the finest, hand - picked platoon of Royal Marine Commandos you or your 'oppos are ever likely to see. As front line troops engaged in very dangerous and arduous missions, we will require certain pre-requisites which you will obtain on our behalf" Then, grinning, "And the first thing you can do is get the bloody kettle on for tea. Now, what's your name?"

"Corporal Bali, Sergeant."

"OK Corporal Bali, your first task will be to continue keeping a

102

guard on this place by day and night, understood? Good. Can't have my specialist troops bothering about guard duties. We'll be out as it is most nights on patrols and ambushes so we must have the maximum rest periods, OK?"

"I understand, Sergeant. Where will you be sleeping though. My men are in the only room at the back?"

"They will move into this office with whoever is on duty. My men need the back room. Every morning at 0700 you are to waken us with tea. Must start the day off properly, eh lads?" he grinned.

"Of course."

"What about breakfast, Sarge?"

"Good point, Laker. When we are getting ready for our hazardous day's duties, your men will knock up some breakfast. OK? Now. as we're going to be seeing a lot of each other I'm sure we can come to some arrangement over supplies. I am prepared to supplement your rations with whatever we can get our mits..... I mean whatever we are supplied with by our Headquarters in return for your co-operation on any problems we may have. Can't be any fairer than that, can I?"

"No Sergeant."

"OK then. So now we'll go and get our gear sorted out while you fetch the tea round when it's ready. Alright?"

"Yes Sergeant. Only one problem. No tea."

"Scouse, get them some from your pack for now. See if they can't rustle up some proper milk, too. That tube stuff gets up my throat."

"OK Sarge. There's probably some in the village somewhere, too. We'll explore the delights of the village shortly. Then we'll get really organised."

"OK. Here you are Lofty, catch." Lee threw a pack of brewing material to one of the Rangers and called him a dummy for dropping it.

Moving around to the back of the building, the platoon stowed their gear around the sizable room which comfortably accommodated all seven of them.

Ten minutes later, the Corporal of the Sarawak Rangers and two of his men banged on the door announcing the arrival of the teas.

"Leave one man on watch in the office and bring yourself and the rest round and join us" said Baron.

"Thank you Sergeant. We don't very often have nice tea like this."

"Well you're going to like this bugger OK. Go and get the rest my son." Then, when the tall slim Ranger had left

"Scouse, pass me that flask you've got in your map pocket."

"What flask, Sarge? I ain't got any booze, honest."

"Don't bullshit me my son. Either that's a bottle in your trousers or the biggest hard on this side of the fuckin' Mississippi. Come, give."

"Eyes like a fuckin' shitehawk" moaned Lee.

"Commando, ain't I?"

"Of course."

"Now, let's give these buggers a cup of Rosy Lea to remember" as he poured a generous tot into each cup.

"What're you trying to do? Blow their fuckin' heads off?"

"They'll be like putty in my hands after this little lot. We'll have a field day here, just as long as we can keep out of Robbo's way. Just think, lads, no guard, tea in the morning, an early warning system in case Robbo comes striding down the road and you can bet these sods know all the best spots in town and where all the goodies are.

"Not just a pretty face, is he?" joked Moran

"Organisation my son; organisation." beamed Baron.

Just then the Rangers returned and seating them down on the floor next to him, Baron poured more teas into their water bottle mugs and handed the others to the Rangers. "Drink up my sons. Cheers."

"Cheers" came the chorus from marines and Rangers alike.

"Don't drink it too fast my sons. You're on duty tonight don't forget. I'll make out a roster for you shortly. Now, what happens in this town?"

"Very quiet town, sir. Nothing happens here. Very peaceful."

"Not for fuckin' long" said Mackay.

"Who lives in all these houses then?" asked Baron.

"The large house at the end of the street is the laundry, sir. Next is the store. Next is the meat shop. Next shop for clothes. All the other buildings are houses for the people. They catch fish from the river and out in the bay. And get fruits from ulu to take into the market at Brunei town to sell. Also grow some crops in field behind houses."

"Bloody grass that'll be"

"Probably smoke themselves stupid, so we'll have to watch that."

"Where do you get your food from then?" asked Lee.

"People in town very generous. Bring us fresh food every day" said a small squat Ranger swilling the last dregs from the mug and holding it out for more. "This very good tea" he grinned.

"So what is your actual job here then?"

"We keep check on river traffic. Border not far away, so some men try to smuggle guns and drugs over border by river. More tea, please."

"Not backward in coming forward, is he?" said Linden sprawled out on the floor.

"Last one, then. My lads have had a very hard day and need sleep after food. Got anything round your side?"

"Today's food gone. More tomorrow."

"OK. Wake us at 0700."

"Yes sir."

"With a nice Rosy Lea, of course."

"Excuse me sir. Who is the lady Rosy Lea?"

"Tea, my son, tea."

"Oh yes indeed, sir. This is cocky slang, no?"

"Quite educated really, ain' he?"

"Cockney slang, my friend, not cocky. I'll teach you some more as the days go by. You'll talk like a real barrow boy by the time I've done with you."

"What is barrow boy, please?"

"Don't worry about it sunshine. See you tomorrow."

Leaving the machine gunners with a big smile on his face, the corporal and his men returned to their office, taking their bundles of sleeping bags and clothing with them.

"Right, lads. We could be on a nice little number here for a while out of the way. Better get that bloody field telephone fixed up before bloody Robbo starts trotting down here to see what we're up to. The less contact we have with him the better. What say you?"

"Too bleedin' true. We'd better not let him know we've got the Rangers on permanent guard duty or he'll find us other things to do like patrols and things." said Mackay.

"Yeah, he won't leave us alone for too long, you watch. What's the betting he'll be down here first thing in the bloody morning."

"No doubt. Anyway, how's about getting some nosh on the go then Lewy?"

"Am I duty chef again then?"

"Shave off, it's only the last few tins we nicked from that village. Surely you can't make a balls up of that?"

"Wanna bet?"

"Good lad. And while you're doing that, we'll sort you out a nice bed space and then I'll read you all a verse or two or ten of dear old Rudyard. Who could ask for more?" smiled Baron.

"I'm going for a shower."

"Think I'll join you."

"You fuckin' won't."

"How about 'Soldier and Sailor Too'?" grinned Baron. "That's my favourite, y'know."

"You don't say?"

"Is that phone fixed up yet Ginger?"

"Almost. Bloody terminals are a bit buggered but it'll do. Try that."

Giving the handle a sharp ring, Baron established contact with the signaller at the Headquarters and was ordered to contact Robson an hour later. Roger.

"He's probably having one of his stuttering bouts and choking on his caviar with a bit of luck" said Moran.

"Don't like him much, do you Moran?"

"Bastard gave me seven days inside once, at Lympstone."

"What for?"

"Screwing a bird in the barrack room one night."

"So what's wrong with that? Everybody does at some time."

"I was on guard duty at the time.

"So how did he catch you?"

"Well, she was one of those stupid birds from Exmouth, typical Janner. Started screaming her head off as she was coming and just as Robbo was going round the block on rounds. He thought someone was getting raped I suppose and burst into the room like fuckin' Audy Murphy."

"What did he say?"

"Went fuckin' spare. I even offered her to him, and that just made him bloody worse 'Get that whore out of the Royal Marine Depot' he cried and woke the whole fuckin' block up. Called me all the bloody lecherous names he could think of. All the lads in the room were pissing themselves at him and that didn't help matters much. So I got seven of the best. But I got the bastard back, in Malta."

"Well, there was this pig's piss up at the officer's club on the beach near Valetta. I was on duty on the roof. We had to flash this bloody great searchlight about every few minutes to make sure no rebels were creeping up to the barbed wire that fenced the beach off outside the pig's bar which was situated right on the shore. All the pigs were in the water with a crowd of nurses and some with their wives. All bloody topless. Typical pig's trash. Even the Padre was at it."

"They're the worst fuckers of all."

"Anyway, I was watching this lot when I saw Robbo in the water with this bit of stuff. She was waving her bra in the air, pissed as a newt. Her old man was in the bar, too and she didn't give a toss. So I see her and Robbo edging towards the shore but coming in on the other side of the wire. They were obviously going to sneak out the outside of the wire and get between the beach huts for a good screw. So I let them get out of the water and start slipping up the beach arm in arm and then I put the searchlight on them. You should've seen them! Robbo didn't know whether to fart, shit or what. All the pigs and their party's looked over to see what the light had picked up."

"What did they do then?"

"Couldn't do fuck all."

"You mean they just stood there?"

"Nah. Robbo, cool as you like after he realised he was in the public eye as it were, just jogged gently back down the beach and into the water. Left the bird stood there all on her tod. Then she panicked and fuckin' near broke the mile record, knockers flowing and bouncing all over the place. Me and the others were pissing ourselves laughing but Robbo couldn't tell just which one of us it was on the light from where he was. Bloody sure he knew it was me though because he must've checked the duty roster, but he couldn't prove it and none of us would've said anything to him."

"So that's why you two don't get on."

"I think, really, he must've seen the funny side to it as well."

"Fucking embarrassing though."

"Nah. Nobody gave a toss out there in those days."

"Nothing's changed then."

"Are we ready for Rudyard now then?" asked Baron, book in hand.

"Have we got a choice?"

"Bit of culture will do you all some good, Now....."

"Answer that Scouser" Baron responded to the ringing of the field telephone.

"For you Sarge"

"Is it who I think it is?" Lee nodded confirmation that Robson was on the other end of the line.

"Yessir, Sergeant Knight speaking. Very good, sir. yessir. Of course not, sir. Good night, sir." And replacing the phone "Hope your balls fester and drop off, sir."

"What's his problem Sarge?" asked Mackay.

"Bloody O Group at 0800 tomorrow morning. Wonder what the bloody hell he's got in store for us now?"

"Probably on the move again."

"Nah, not that quick. Must be a patrol or something." Bright and early they were duly shaken by the Rangers with tea as requested and after showering and cleaning their weapons and a sparse breakfast of more tea and hard tack biscuits, Baron trooped off up the hill to the O Group. As he and Linden passed through the length of the village they noticed that all the people that they passed waved and greeted them and, had they more time, Baron would have accepted the seemingly warm invitations to enter some of the houses and sample the hospitality. But they were already a few minutes late and rather than incur Robbo's wrath any more than necessary they pushed on.

Meanwhile, the remainder of the platoon, under MacKay, cleaned the police station out with the aid of the Rangers who naturally did most of the work, and waited for their leader's return.

The consequence of the O Group was that Baron and the MMGs had been given a virtually free hand to patrol their immediate area and report any unusual occurrences with special emphasis on the river traffic. They would be informed of any other duties they were to perform and of when to collect rations and supplies and mail. And no, there was no news of Lee or Lewis being repatriated in the near future.

"We're here for bloody life. That lot in Drafting couldn't organise a piss up in a brewery or a bun fight in a bakery. Useless bastards."

"Never mind, lads. Just think of all that money that's piling up in the bank. You'll be worth a fortune soon. And what could be better than spending a nice relaxing holiday by a beautiful river, surrounded by nature at its best?" laughed Baron.

"One night in the Spotlight, pissed as a rat; then a good bagoff with a Nee Soon Virgin. That's what."

"I bet bloody Tug Wilson is in UK now. Most likely down Guz swimming in scrumpy in the London Bar down Union Strazza."

"Yeah. Then it'll be up the Prince Regent, pick up a scrubber, whip her up the Hoe and show bloody Drake what he really should've done with his balls."

As expected, Robson blessed them with his presence the next day with orders that they were to set forth immediately on a patrol into the jungle to a kampong five miles from their location, purely as an exercise to let the locals know that they were in the vicinity. They were to make contact with as many habitations within a five mile radius of Trusan as possible in the hope that information may be gleaned on any gun running activities or movement of rebel forces in the area.

These orders Baron found an inconvenience as it had been his intention that day to have an in depth sortie of the town with the object of 'organising' a few supplies for his men and really getting to know the locals. But that would have to wait now.

"Don't worry, sir. We'll sort them out."

"Christ. I don't want anyone 'sorting out' Sergeant. Just show the flag, humour them, try and gain their confidence. Then we may possibly get some valuable information from them at a later stage. Understand?"

"Clear as a bell, sir."

"Carry on Sergeant. Bloody hell, why did I get landed like this?"

"Right lads. Five minutes to get booted and spurred. Patrol rig."

"It's OK Sarge. He's gone now."

"Sure?"

"Yeah."

"Ok. Get the kettle on then Lewy. Time for a quick brew before we fuck off. Bloody nuisance. I had plans for today." Leaving Trusan behind, with the Rangers in control at the station, the platoon set off at a leisurely pace through the sparse outskirts of the jungle at the end of the village. A crisp, clear morning, the jungle steamed as the sun streamed through the tree tops onto the sodden ground below.

"It's going to be fucking hot today, Scouse."

"Yeah, but it's only five miles to the kampong, so it shouldn't be so bad, unless our great leader makes a fuck up with his map reading."

"I heard that, Lee. Have no fear my sons. It's more or less a straight line from here to there. All we got to do is run parallel to the river. No problem. Piece of piss." The further they penetrated the jungle, the thicker it became and soon the marines were bathed in sweat which rose from their bodies in thick steam. And smelt. Hacking a path through the thick foliage with their machete's the machine gunners became tensely aware that this was virgin territory to them and they steeled themselves for the slightest indication of an attack. But none was forthcoming and as they reached a clearing at the intersection of two paths Baron called a halt and permitted them to smoke while he consulted his map and decided that the kampong was barely half a mile away now.

"Out pipes. Let's go lads."

"Bury your dog-ends, too before we move out. Don't want any bastard picking up our trail too quickly." said the ever cautious Mackay.

Following one of the paths in a southerly direction now, they shortly came to the last of the thick jungle and into a large expanse of flat tree-less farm land abundantly covered with a crop which Laker assured them was wheat. Or barley. Or oats. Or something like that.

The path ran down about two hundred yards to two buildings situated centrally amongst the fields. One was obviously a barn of some description and the other an exquisitely thatched long, log cabin styled building which appeared totally out of place stuck in the middle of nowhere.

At the edge of the jungle the marines cautiously scanned the area keeping a wary eye on the dozen or so natives working in the fields ahead of them earnestly engaged in cutting and stacking the crops.

"Harvest time, obviously" whispered Mackay.

"Must be some rich bastard that owns this little lot, eh?"

"Yeah. Hold on, what's happening now?"

"Must be lunch break. They all seem to be heading for the house."

"We'll wait until they're all in there and then pay them a little visit, I reckon."

"Catch then on the hops, as it were Sarge, eh?" grinned Mackay.

"Oh, very droll. You should have been on the stage; it left just now."

"Oi, you two. Bloody Laurel and Hardy. What's the score?" called Moran from behind.

"We're going to do a spot of visitations, my sons. See those two places over there? Right, well that's where we're headed.

"What is it, a farm?"

"Ten for observation, Ginge."

"My uncle had a farm in Wolverhampton, once" said Laker.

"How the fuck can you have a farm in the middle of bleedin' Wolverhampton?"

"You could before they built the motorway."

"What sort of farm was it?"

"Well, it was a funny sort of place, really."

"Just the place you ought to be, a bloody Funny Farm" laughed Lewis.

"Bollicks. Anyway, he had this bloody great sow and me and my cousin used to let it out now and again, for a laugh. The bloody thing used to run like fuck up the road to a factory and scare the shit out of the factory bints. One day they caught the bastard and took it up to the abattoir, knocked it on the head and took it back to the factory. They were all stuffing themselves rotten on it when my uncle found out. He went bleedin' spare. It was worth a few bob apparently. Won a few prizes at the shows. Tasted nice though."

"Well, thank you for that thrilling insight to life in rural Wolverhampton. Now, would anybody mind too much if we got back to being bloody Royal Marines on active service?" said Baron.

"I reckon if we split in two and each take one side of the path through the wheat or whatever it is, we can virtually get to the front door without being seen" said MacKay.

"My thoughts exactly" Baron replied.

"I'll take the right side with Linden, Moran and Laker then, and you and the others take the left, OK?"

"Spot on. Make a Sergeant of you yet, my son" grinned Baron.

Slipping from the jungle into the field in their two groups, the patrol advanced to within twenty yards of the buildings before they were spotted by two women who had emerged from the barn. Standing there laughing and grinning to themselves, the smaller and prettier of the two pointed at the Baron's group.

Seeing that they had blown their cover, Baron stepped from the field and onto the track.

"What the fuckin' hell are they laughing at?" asked Lee who, like the rest was covered from head to toe in the small darts of barley and to the amusement of the girls resembled the scarecrows that were dotted all over the farm.

"Buggered if I know."

"Why you not use path?" called the smaller girl. grinning at them.

"Much easier" called the other, taller and very thin.

"Ever felt like a spare prick at a pro's wedding?" asked Lee.

"OK lads" called Baron to the other group. "All round observation until we see what this lot's all about."

"You want tea, Johnny? Or maybe something stronger?" said the tall girl.

"Hang about darlin'. Let's just have a little butchers at what's inside first. Jock, take your lot over to the barn and give it a going over. And the farm hands. Ginge, you and Scouse stay out here and keep a watch out. Lewy. come with me into the house. Let's go." Warily entering the log cabin, the marines immediately saw that this was no ordinary basher. On the inside, the walls were covered with large and very beautiful silk embroideries, in the centre of which were two large portraits of Her Majesty the Queen and Prince Phillip. The furniture in the reception area was of the finest hand carved wood, polished to a degree they had not seen before. Large silk cushions were strewn about the floor and in one corner there was a bar and an expensive looking hi-fi.

"Jesus Christ" breathed Lewis.

"Fuck my old sea boots" said Baron.

"That could be pretty close to the mark, if I'm not mistaken."

"Yeah. Check the other rooms. See if they're anything like these."

"You know what this looks like, don't you?"

"Yeah. The local knocking shop par excellence."

"Correct."

"Here Sarge, look at this little lot" exclaimed Lewis as he returned from one of the rooms, his arms full of magazines and papers.

"What's that, enemy propaganda again?"

"Enemy propaganda my arse. These bastard make Penthouse look like the fuckin' Beano. Cop this."

"Never mind the literature. Where's the real thing, that's what I want to know."

"Hey, missie. Where all pretty girls, then?" shouted Lewis.

"Girls come tonight. You come back tonight. Me get you best girls in whole Borneo." she smiled.

Just then Mackay and the others entered the room. "What's new then Sarge?"

"Get a butchers at this lot" called Lewis.

"Shave off. Plenty of wanking material here" said Laker.

"Better still, the real thing's on hand" said Lewis.

"Where? Lead me to it" replied Lee.

"What time do girls get here?" asked Baron.

"Six o'clock. Everyone come after six o'clock."

"I bet they do" laughed Lee.

"Have velly good time." smiled the girl.

"Well, there might just be enough here to keep me going to six." said Lee wandering over to the bar and helping himself to a large tot of brandy wine.

"Forget it, Scouse and the rest of you" said Baron. "There' no way we're hanging around here until six. It'll be bloody dark then and we're a long way from home. We'd never find our way back in the dark, in any case."

"Better stay the night, then hadn't we?"

"And just what do you think friend Robbo would say to that?"

"He'd probably send half the bloody combined forces out for us."

"Think so? No, he'd be only too glad to have us off his back." "Wouldn't give a toss."

"Either way, we'll never know 'cos we're off as soon as we've freshened up a bit and had a rest."

"Come on Sarge, they won't miss us, will they?" pleaded Lee.

"Don't you believe it, and leave that booze alone. I'm not carrying you all the bloody way back."

"Just leave me here for a day or two with all these birds and this bar full of booze. It's like an oasis, eh?"

"Don't tempt me Scouser. You're a piss head and a sex maniac. How long do you think these poor young virgins will last with you at them every five minutes?"

"They'll all be syphed up to the bloody eyeballs, and anyway, Scouse we don't want a dose before repat, do we?" piped in Mackay.

" I'll take my chances."

"Besides, we haven't seen what the local talent is like yet. have we?"

"Might be as rough as fuck for all we know."

"If they're anything like these parties in this magazine......."

"Just when have you seen any talent like that running around bloody Borneo?"

"All I've seen in bloody Borneo is ulu, mossies, rivers, bootnecks and pusser's bloody hardtack."

"Cut it out, you two. We're not stopping and that's that. Let's get back outside and see what there is around."

"Nothing in the barn Sarge. All the labourers' are sat round a long table noshing. They're no bother. Quite friendly really."

"Any talent amongst them?" asked Lee.

"Nothing that would interest even you, my old Scouse."

"I don't know. Those two who took the piss out of us might be candidates for the thrill of their little lifetimes."

"Hark at bloody Valentino.

"You've either got it or you haven't. If you've got it , you get it; if you haven't , tough shit, Royal Marines."

"Where's the tea and scones then darlin'?"

"Please?"

"Never mind. Just the tea will be OK. And, of course, a little drop of something to warm it up a bit, eh?" he grinned.

"Please to all go in house now. We fetch tea and brandy wine for honoured guests."

"Yeah, and maybe half the bloody Indonesian army. Lakes and Moran stay out here and keep watch. We'll relieve you in a while. Don't let anyone slide off into the ulu or anywhere else, OK?"

"Right 'O' Sarge. Bring us out a wet though before you get too pissed to remember us."

"OK"

While the others draped themselves over the furniture Baron sprawled out on the floor amongst a pile of cushions.

"Just like home, this lads. All I need now is the missus and the kids jumping all over me. If fuckin' Robbo saw us now, he'd jump over the lot of us."

"Rhodesian git."

"He could be worse."

"Not much."

"Pass that bottle over Lewy."

"Nothing worth nicking here then?"

"Not unless you'd like to carry that bloody furniture back to Trusan."

"Perhaps we'll borrow a few of their literary gems."

"Not a bad way to fight the war, eh, lads?" said Baron

"I could quite easily flake out here for a few weeks with a young virgin or two."

"You wouldn't know a virgin if you fell over one."

"Yeah. I picked up this bird down the Fez Bar in Pompey once. Just got out of training I had. I was paralytic. Pissed as a newt. She told me she was a virgin and she said I could take her home. She was getting better looking with every pint, so I waltzes her up the road to the Married Quarters at Eastney - I should've twigged then, really - and turns in with it. Fuck me, next morning there's five kids jumping all over the bleeding bed shouting 'Daddy, Daddy."

"So what did you do?"

"She sent them down to the park, and I kept me head under the bed clothes until they'd gone. Just as well 'cos even after a wash and some makeup she was as rough as fuck. I grabbed me gear and fucked off a bit smartish. Thank fuck I was on draft the next day."

"Do you own this place then?" Mackay asked one of the women.

"Father own farm. Today go to market for food and cattle sale."

"Would you like me to do you a favour?" asked Lee.

"The booze is finally taking effect, I see."

"Shut up Scouse. You and Lewy go and relieve the other two."

"I was only kidding."

"I'm not. Go"

"Any soldiers come this way?" asked Baron.

"You first soldiers we see. No more."

"Wouldn't tell us if they did, would you darling?"

"Me very honest. Me good girl."

"I'm sure. Anyway, got to keep Robbo happy by asking, eh?" laughed Baron.

After they had all taken a turn on guard duty, Baron decided that they must move off before they got too pissed or before it got dark. Reluctantly , they left, but vowed to return when they could.

Now they had to push hard for Trusan before darkness fell and apart from both Moran and Laker heaving up as a result of their over - indulgences, their journey back proved uneventful and they reached the station just as dusk fell.

"I'd better give bloody Robbo a bell and tell him we're back in the fold. The sod won't believe we've been chasing around from kampong to kampong, anyway, but best to go through the motions, eh?" smiled Baron.

"Yessir, that's right, four kampongs we searched. No, nothing of any interest, sir. Very hard going though. The jungle is very thick once you get out of the village, quite shattering, really. We're all quite done in, as it were, sir. No sir, all back in one piece, you'll be pleased to hear. Oh really? Thank you, hic, sir. Sorry, sir. Spot of indigestion. OK, sir. Goodnight, sir."

"And, the fucking idiot really thought we'd been grafting today. The silly sod has given us a virtual day off tomorrow for 'administration' in view of the surprising amount of ground your platoon covered today'

"Bloody nice of him. What's he after?"

"Probably he's gone bent after all this time in the jungle and he's after Barons' parts." laughed Lee.

"Your mind is fuckin' warped, Scouser."

"Wait until you've been out here as long as we have. You'll go bloody warped as well."

"Come on my ansomes, let's have three of you for a hand or two of bridge, then, Lewy, Jock, Ginge, OK?"

"Is this instead of bloody Rudyard?" asked MacKay.

"No, my son, he comes afterwards" beamed Baron.

"I suppose that leaves the rest of us to get the grub for tonight, does it?" asked Laker.

"Nothing like a good volunteer, is there?" grinned Baron.

"Answer that bugger somebody."

"Bloody hell, what's going on?"

"The bleedin' phone's on the go. Can't you hear it?"

"What time is it?"

"One o'clock."

"Fucking hell, Can't those bastards sleep up there?"

"MMGs. Marine Laker speaking. Who? Oh, sorry sir. Can I help you, sir? Sergeant who? Oh, yes. Hang on. Sir. I'll wake him up. Sir. Put the bloody lights on. Where's Baron? Can't see a bloody thing. He's over in the corner ain't he? Shake him somebody, for Chrissake. Bloody Robbos's blowing his haystack, here. Come on Sarge it's the Rhodesian Rat on the blower. Just coming, sir."

"Wake up Sarge, Robbo's on the dog and bone."

"Tell 'im to piss off. I need my beauty sleep. What time is it?"

"Sergeant Knight said to, sir, ..."

"Laker! Shut up."

"Thought that would make you move Sarge" grinned Laker in the half light provided by the candle Mackey had lit."

"Morning , sir. Yessir. Yessir. Yessir. Clear as a bell, sir. Thank you sir. Goodnight sir." And, as he put the phone down. "Piss off, sir."

"Right, then. Rise and shine my ansomes. We've got a little job to do."

"At this time of night? You must be bloody joking."

"Wish I was."

"Shave off. No bloody peace for the wicked, is there?"

"Apparently the big boys up top have got a buzz that there could be some troop movements through this area at any moment so we've got to get out and lay a few booby traps for them on the paths leading into town from this end. The others are looking after the other end. So come then, let's get a move on, then we can get our bloody heads down again. Gash rig and weapons, of course. We'll need half a dozen grenades and wire and a few flares. Remind me to make sure the coppers shake us before dawn so we can defuse the snares before the bloody locals start tramping about in the morning. I expect some bugger will decide to wander about before the curfew is lifted and blow himself to smithereens. But that's their hard shit. They've been warned. Bring a couple of torches, Jock. Everyone ready then? Come on Lakes, last again."

"Can't find one of me bleedin' Jungle Boots."

"Hurry up, Lakes."

"It was 'ere when I got me 'ead down."

"So think. Where were you when you took your boots off?"

"Right here. Oh, yeah. Its 's alright, I've got it."

"What the hell was it doing in your sleeping bag?"

"Well, I thought if they're in the bag then firstly I'll know exactly where they are if I need to get rigged in a hurry, and secondly it keeps them out of the way of all the weirdies that like sleeping in them."

"No self respecting weirdy would go within a hundred yards of your bloody boots, anyway."

"Balls." Filtering out of the station, the disgruntled marines made their way to the edge of town and the tracks they were to set up the booby traps on. There were two standard methods of setting up a pathway, firstly by means of a trip wire connected to a stake on one end and the firing pin of a grenade on the other. So as a person fell over the trip wire the grenade exploded. The other method they used was to incorporate a signal flare into the same trip wire so that with a reversible switch they could actually, if they were around that is, watch their victims blow themselves up. This method was more often used in ambushes but tonight they had no intention of lying in wait for anybody. In less than an hour their traps were complete and they returned to the station.

"Perhaps we can get our bloody heads down now."

"Not for long my ansomes. Someone's got to disarm them in three hours time and we'll have to do this every day and night now, too, you watch."

"For our own protection, I suppose." said Mackay.

"I'll work out a roster" continued Baron. "Me and Jock will disarm them this morning so you lot can sleep in heavenly peace, my sons."

"So you can wake us with the tea then, Sarge."

"Yeah , alright then, I'll be duty chef tomorrow for breakfast, at least. What's it to be then? Toast lightly done on both sides? Eggs boiled, poached, scrambled or fried? Fruit juice? Medium grilled kidneys? Perhaps a starter of iced Melon or Grapefruit lightly sprinkled with sugar?"

"How about Pusser's hard tack and stewed tea, as usual?"

"Why didn't I think of that? Anyone fancy an ode or two before you nod off?"

"Piss off."

"Thought you might say that."

"Rise and shine my beauties. Tea up. Hands off cocks, on socks. Don't roll over, roll out. It's a lovely day and we've got nothing to do but get organised. Organisation......"

"Give it a rest, for Chrissake. Why do I get a shake every time I'm about to give someone the thrill of a lifetime?" moaned Lee.

"You could just about give No-nose a thrill up her one and only left nostril"

"Charming. First thing in the bloody morning and woken up to bloody No-nose's left nostril."

"Right, lads, after brekky and a good weapon check we'll make a move. First of all I want one volunteer to stay here in the station with the Rangers in case Robbo calls us on the blower while the rest of us go and have a little looksee around the town or village, rather and see if we can get something organised with the locals. Like some decent nosh."

"OK Sarge, I'll stay" said Mackay. "If it's alright with you, that is. Got a couple of letters to write, including the old woman. I haven't written to her for a month so I'm due for a bollicking as it is."

"That's fine, Jock. Right, the rest, get your weapons cleaned and then we can piss off."

"Can't we go back to that farm brothel Sarge?" asked Lee.

"Another day, my son, another day."

"Pity, I could just do with a good bagoff."

"You could always do with a good bagoff, randy sod."

"A mere healthy lust" grinned Lee.

"I think we'll start at the laundry. There seems to be plenty of activity there. Come on, let's go."

Crossing the road, the group made their way the short distance to the large laundry building which was indeed, a hive of activity. A dozen or so lines of brightly coloured washing hung outside in a clearing immediately in front of the jungle edge and four very young Malay girls, teenagers they guessed, busied themselves taking in and hanging out all the different articles.

"There's a fair bit of talent here, right on our bloody doorstep. No need to go on patrols now, eh?" said Lee.

"That's about as far as your observation limits go, ain't it Scouse" said Laker.

"You'd better get back to UK quick before you bust a gut or something."

"Don't tell me you wouldn't crawl through some of them if you got the chance. Lakes."

"Don't know if I'd trust my chopper with one of them. Probably all got black syph or worse."

"Hadn't we better start thinking about the grub aspect of things" interrupted Baron.

"You sex maniacs think of nothing but dipping your wicks. How about the other things in life, like food glorious food?"

"You must've been young once Sarge" said Lee, grinning.

"Cheeky little bastard. For that you can stand guard outside and keep a sharp lookout. And keep your dirty hands off the locals."

"Don't forget me, though, will you?"

"As if we could. Hello mama" Baron greeted the large rotund woman who appeared at the entrance to the laundry. "Nice little firm you've got here. Who's dhobi is all this then?"

"What dhobi, boss?"

"Washing. All this clobber. Where does it come from?"

"This all come from town ten miles away. That way" she said pointing due north towards the opposite end of town. "Come and go from the river. Velly good business. Make plenty dollars, but me have to pay girls, so me not rich lady, like soldiers."

"Pull this bugger, darling, it's got bells on it."

"Bells?"

"Forget it. Don't mind if we have a little looksee round your place, do you mama?"

"Yes , please to come in house. I make for you tea. Velly good tea for velly good soldiers."

"Marines, not bleeding pongos" said Luther.

"Corps pissed all of the sudden aren't we?"

"Why not? Must educate the natives, eh?"

"Please" the woman said, "What Pongo?"

"Just a rabble called the army. Don't worry about it, darlin'."

"How many more girlies work here?" said Baron.

"Four at back do washing by stream. Good girls." said the woman.

"I'll inspect them Sarge, OK?" said Moran.

"Take Lewy with you. And behave yourselves you two buggers." Passing through the house Moran and Lewis soon found themselves out back where barely twenty yards to their front the four women were pummelling away at a large container full of clothing with long poles with what appeared to be boxing gloves at the end of each. The receptacles were filled almost to the top with hot water and the girls were standing on boxes three feet high so they were able to punch down on the clothes.

"Look at the tonsils on that one, Lewy" gasped Moran. "I could give her one. Or two."

"Down, Rover. Pretty though, ain't they?"

"Hello darling. Wanna wash my kecks out? You'll have to come and take them off first though. Whadda ya laughing at?"

Resplendent in their gaily coloured sarongs the girls clearly wore absolutely nothing beneath them and their firm young bodies strained against the tight fitting material, as the two marines took in every detail in earnest.

"I think that one with the big knockers fancies me. Lewy"

"Dream along with me" his partner sang "I'm on my way to the stars"

"No, straight up She keeps smiling at me, the little cracker."

"Don't tell me. You're in love again."

"Well, I wouldn't go quite that far. Yet."

"C'mon, we'd better get back inside. Baron will be out here in a minute to see what we're up to."

"Hang about, I'm sure she wants my body."

"She looks fed up, not hard up."

"Don't try and deny the girl the moment she's been waiting for all her life."

"What are you two up to then?" called Baron standing at the doorway.

"Nothing, Sarge. We were just coming in. Nothing out of order here."

"Come on then, the tea's ready and that mama has laced it suitably with some brandy wine. Even she is starting to look quite tasty" he grinned.

"You two carry on" said Moran. I'll be right with you. Just going for a quick crap in the ulu. Won't be a minute."

"Why don't you nip back to the station?" asked Baron. "It's much more comfortable than getting your arse full of the weirdies crawling around the ulu."

"Yeah, OK then. I'll go round the side way, save going through the house."

"Have you got any food organised then Sarge?"

"Patience, my son. Just wait and watch and listen. And learn."

"Now what's he up to?"

"Mama, you very beautiful lady. Me likee you velly much."

"Jesus Christ."

"Me likee Sergeant. Velly handsome marine." she grinned back, bowing almost to the floor.

"What's this then, a bloody mutual admiration society?"

"OK mama. Perhaps some more light refreshment while we wait?" said Baron offering his glass to the woman.

"Oh yes. Of course. I fetch. Tell girl to cook food now. Back soon."

"Go with her Ginge."

"I read your mind. Just about to."

"Well, here we are again, lads, organised to fuck. Your leader has done it again" said Baron stretching back in a chair that hardly seemed capable of holding his mighty frame.

"Yeah, gotta hand it to you again Sarge" said Luther swigging back the last of his glass of brandy wine. "I could damn soon get shot away on this stuff, too" he said looking appreciatively at the glass, as one of the girls refilled it.

"Pity we can't get this stuff in Guz, eh?" said Moran. "Imagine mixing this stuff with scrumpy. Knock your bleedin' head off."

"Talking of scrumpy reminds me of a time I was down there as a young corporal" said Baron.

"Swing that fuckin' lamp somebody. It's memoirs time again."

"Bloody funny it was. I was with the Mortars then, and we had to do a manpack march over the moors from dear old Bickleigh. That was when it was just a transit and Commando training camp. Rough as fuck in those days. So, we set off this day to cover all these check points we had to stop at. Course, between every point there was a few farms and all these bloody Janner farmers have got their own bloody scrumpy factory in the barn. Needless to say, we didn't quite make it to the final checkpoint; in fact, out of seven, we only made three, and then only because we got a lift on a hay wagon to the last one. So the bloody pig in charge of the platoon got in a panic and thought we'd got lost on the moor. What made it worse was that the bloody mist came down and you all know what that's like on the moor. Anyway, this pig gets all up the shit and radios the emergency services. Christ, it was just like when one of the prisoners escapes from Dartmoor prison, police and troops all over the place. In the end they got a bloody chopper from the Naval Air Station down Culdrose out as well."

"Did they find you in the end?"

"No chance. We were in the barn of this farm as pissed as rats with the farmer and his missus. By the centre, she could drink, too. Must've been weaned on the stuff. In the end he took us back to camp on his tractor and trailer. Fucking platoon officer went bleedin' bananas. Set my promotion back a few years, too. And his." Baron giggled.

"Food coming now Sergeant, sir."

"Ah, damn fine show, Carruthers" mimicked Baron. "Where's the dancing girls then? Must have some cabaret."

"This lot looks alright eh?" Laying out a huge bowl of rice with spices and chopped meat on the table before the marines, the mama gave each one a large plate and a fork and invited them to help themselves. Little invitation was required.

"Just like a nasi goreng down the Spotlight, ain't it?"

"Fucking sight cheaper, too."

"Tomorrow we'll bring her over some Pusser's makings in return."

"What are you going to do? Try and kill them?"

"One more plate for the other Marine, Sergeant. Where he go?"

"Bloody hell, where's Laker got to?"

"Went for a crap, didn't he?"

"Must be the longest crap in history, then. Better go and find the bugger, I suppose." Hardly had the words left Baron's mouth when, sweating profusely, a wry grin on his face. Laker stood in the doorway adjusting his belt and tucking in his jungle green shirt.

"Where the bloody hell have you been?"

"Cementing relations, Sarge" he grinned.

"Bloody hell. Not that one...."

"The same. Told you she thought I was essence. Told her all about my uncle's farm in Wolverhampton and she was mine for the taking."

"Can't leave you alone for five minutes, can we? You realise you've more than likely picked up a lethal dose of clap?"

"Nah, she was very clean. Had a wash before and afterwards. Well, she jumped in the bloody river, anyway."

"Lookout bloody Wolverhampton when he gets back. Grab a plate and get stuck into this lot if you've got the strength left."

"Great. Nothing like a good nosh after a good bagoff. Pass the wine please, waiter" he grinned.

"If your bloody missus could see you now, Sarge, she'd have a fit."

"Nah, she'd understand. Gotta take your chances when you get them, eh?"

"How about those seven kids then? What's that, one for every draft?"

"Just about. Could be more after this little lot though. She hasn't been in Singers long. Not like Malta though."

"What's so special about Malta then?"

"That place used to be the best run ashore in the world at one time. My Christ, a run ashore down the Gut was an experience not to be missed. I remember the day practically the whole Corps ran amok down there." he grinned. "That was really something."

"What happened?"

"Well, some bloody Malt had goffered one of our lads with a bottle. Nothing very unusual, but for some reason everyone thought it about time the Malts got sorted out. It was becoming too much of a habit. So the whole of 40 Commando met up with 42 Commando who'd just pulled into Malta on a carrier and the whole fucking lot marched on the Gut. They totally wrecked the place. Marched from one end to the other and smashed everyone and everything in sight. Nobody went near them, not even the bloody MPs. The Malts shit themselves. But they got the message OK. There were no more problems with them after that. Mind you, the next day the whole of the British Fleet, with both units on board was put to sea, just to keep them out of Malta until it cooled down at bit."

"No wonder Minto wants us out of there."

"Yeah."

"Are we going any further up the town to have a look around, Sarge?"

"Are you joking? If every basher treats us like this, we'll be here forever. It'll take us a month to get to the other end. Besides, I'm full of nosh and Brandy Wine, so who needs to go any further?"

"Let's hope Robbo doesn't take it into his head to come and look for us, or we'll be for it."

"Fuck Robbo. He's only got a few months to do anyway, so he won't want too much of the spotlight."

"Wish to Christ I was in The Spotlight right now."

"So do I."

"All that bagging off and pissing up ain't no good for you. Wait 'til you get hitched and got a few kids. Then you gotta think about the money. The kids always need new clothes and the missus is always screaming for some new rags. That's where all the responsibility starts coming in and all the money starts going out. You don't have a spare penny to yourself, so you grab it where you can"

"I couldn't handle being married yet. Fancy being restricted by a bloody woman." said Lewis.

"OK, but think of those cold nights at Bickeigh camp when the snow's on the ground and you're on your own when you could be tucked up with a good woman. Or a bad woman in your case" laughed Baron.

"Doesn't make up for the freedom a man gets when he wants to go out on the piss with his mates though."

"Yeah, but as you get older, you'll change, you'll see."

"It was bloody funny the last time I was at Bickleigh" said Moran who, as a slightly longer serving marine had served in most of the units including those on shore bases, in UK that were referred to as 'Stonewall Frigates'." Bickleigh was one such camp, in Plymouth on the edge of Dartmoor. "You remember those old Nissen huts don't you Sarge, all tin and sod all else?"

"Do I ever....."

"Well, when I first got a draft there as a sprog just after training, it was just before Christmas. I couldn't for the life of me understand why all the old soldiers had volunteered for rear-party over the leave period. Fuck me, the next Christmas I got put on rear party myself and bloody soon found out! The whole unit used to be formed up on the parade and marched all the way down to that little station, remember

Sarge? And stuck on the train to Plymouth Main Line station for the connections up country. Well, fuck me, if on the very next train to arrive back at Bickleigh, all the bleedin' pros from Union Street with their suitcases and everything moved into the barracks. There was about fifty of them, one each for the rear-party. Then another load arrived on the bus when that pulled in. You couldn't move for bloody women. Mind you, they were a bit on the rough side, but who cares when it's freezing cold in the middle of bloody Dartmoor over Xmas? Every time you went for a piss or a shower there was some bird in there. They used to moan like fuck if you interrupted them, too."

"Then there was the sheep and wild ponies that used to roam around the camp all the time. Sometimes those buggers would get into the rooms at night and scare the crap out of you when you wake up in the middle of the night. Add to that lot the rusty water, the old coal fires that were stuck in the middle of each room and the snow and mist that seemed to be always over Bickleigh, and you can imagine the type of paradise that place was."

"Must've been hell" chided Luther.

"You can take the piss, but that was when they needed them, not feeded them" replied Moran. "Bloody camp and a half that was. Good laugh though, sometimes."

"We were at Bickleigh after the Heavy Weapons course, eh, Scouse?" said Lewis.

"Yeah, that was when that bastard Libby was an instructor there. Everybody hated that sod. Right arseole."

"He was so unpopular that when we used to do training on the guns he would check every round on a drill belt to make sure no bugger had slipped a live sod in there. And this was on drill weapons that didn't have a bloody firing pin anyway."

"If you made a cock up on stoppages training, y'know like when they blindfold you and set up a stoppage and you've got a couple of seconds to clear it, then this bastard Libby would load the complete gun on your back and make you run right round the bloody camp, about half a bleedin' mile. And with over a hundred pounds on your back, with no manpack, you soon got bloody knackered."

"Wonder what happened to him?"

"I heard he got killed in a car crash near Culdrose"

"What a shame."

"Talking of Culdrose, we had a bloody good time there, didn't we Scouse?" said Lewis.

"Not many, Benny. We were down there for a fortnight beating up for the Royal Tournament; running up cliffs and attacking radio stations and all that crap. We trained down at Lands End and all round the Cornwall coast. But then Culdrose was full of Wrens and it was like a bloody knocking shop. It was May and the bloody weather was like the Costa Brava, so all the local birds were on the beaches at the weekends as well. You couldn't go wrong. Unless your name was Lewis, of course, and you got caught in the Wrens Quarters in the middle of the night. Not just the Wrens Quarters, but the Wren Officers Quarters. I'd chatted up this little charmer in the all ranks club, then she went to get her head down. Thought I'd give her a break as she was on duty very early the next day, but a couple of hours later the old dick took charge, with a little bit of help from the scrumpy, too, and I decided to pay her a little visit. Being pissed, I was incapable of finding her in the dark, so I put the light on and woke up the fucking lot of them. All in their little baby dolls. Then this big Butch thing grabbed hold of me, ripped my dog-tags off and threw me out the door like I was a bit of shit. Bitch. I got three days stoppage for that."

"Right my ansomes. let's get moving then" beamed Baron. "Enough of these old war stories."

"Do we have to Sarge? That party is looking as though she wants me to do her another favour" called Laker.

"Are you trying to take over as the platoon stallion from Lee?" asked Baron.

"I have my moments" laughed Laker.

"Well this isn't one of them. Get your arse mobile" said Baron.

"Time we had a look at that store place along the road. Got to get a few goodies in just in case they completely forget all about us up there."

"Wish to Christ they would. We'd be better off on our own! Leaving with much bowing and mutterings of thanks and promises of return visits the marines filed out and moved along the couple of doors to the General Store.

"I'm fucked" said Laker.

"Too much bagging off. Just wait until you start pissing razor blades" laughed Lee.

"Balls, she was as clean as a whistle. I hope."

"This is it lads, let's have a butchers" said Baron taking the two steps up to the entrance to the store where he was greeted by the thin, wiry, smiling owner.

"Very happy day Sergeant Baron" the coolie smiled.

"How the bloody hell does he know my name?" asked a startled Baron.

"Probably been listening outside the door all day" said Lewis pointing back to the previous hut.

"Last house and laundry owned by my cousin" the stooping Malay replied.

"Sounds like the Borneo Mafia to me" said Moran.

"Anyway, old chap, we need some supplies. Mind if we take a looksee if there's anything here we could use?"

"Please to take anything honourable marines need" smiled the owner bowing again almost to the floor.

"That lot'll do for a kick off" said Baron eyeing the rows of shelves containing various meats and fish dishes in cans, "Grab as many of them as you can, but leave the bugger a few or he'll get upset." Loading up all that they thought it advisable to take without upsetting the man too much, Baron signed the inevitable chitty and they made their way back to the station, where Mackay was sound asleep.

Waking Mackay was not a safe thing to do. Mackay was apt to come out of a deep sleep swinging his fists at anything within reach and the platoon had long since reverted to poking him with the end of a long stick or a rifle.

"What time is it?" yawned Mackay, sitting up.

"Time you got the tea on" called Baron.

"Oh yeah. Robbo wants you to call him as soon as you get back"

"Well, I'm not back yet, am I?

"Sure."

"Wonder what the bloody hell he wants now?

"Only one way to find out Sarge."

"Yeah, but he can bloody wait until I've had a wet."

"Patrol again tomorrow, lads. Looks like only a four mile trek each way, so not too bad."

"Anywhere near that other kampong?" asked Lee.

"No, so don't go getting bloody excited, Scouser." grinned Baron.

"Better get our heads down now then and sleep the booze off ready for the morning" said Mackay stretching his large, long frame out on the floor.

"Christ, you've only just got up" said Moran.

"Aye, and I'm only just going back to Noddy land. Goodnight all."

"He could sleep on a bloody toothpick" laughed Baron.

"This looks like the place." Mackay said to Baron as they crawled on all fours through the last piece of jungle between them and a small circle of bashers to their front.

"According to the bloody map it is, anyway. Lets have a little butchers. Take Lakes and Ginge and Moran over to the far side, put one of them on stopper in case some bastard makes a break for it, and the rest of us will come in from this end. Search those two bashers at your end and we'll take care of these three between us. We'll meet you in the middle, OK?

"Right you are Sarge. You heard, lads. Let's go." Breaking their cover, the two groups emerged and remained unnoticed until MacKay's group were almost at the other end of the kampong when a small child confronted them almost head-on and ran back into her basher shouting excitedly. Soon, the whole populace was outside staring at the marines. Four older men, six women and a handful of children chattered excitedly without the slightest fear as the marines started to search the bashers.

"Ave a look in that basher while I check this one. Go on you two get a move on. What the hell are you waiting for?" asked Baron."Have you seen that bit of stuff over there, Sarge?" asked Lee staring at one of the women who was leaning seductively on one post of a basher opposite them.

"Shouldn't I go and interrogate her for a while? Might be some useful information there."

Treasure Trove

❝Bullshit. I'll take care of her later. Get bloody moving."

"Yeah, c'mon Scouse, let's see what we can dig out of here."

"Piss all as usual, I expect."

"Careful, there may be some big hairy mama waiting for you."

"That'll be the day."

As they entered the basher, the old wizened woman who lived in it tried to follow them in but she was soon dissuaded from doing so by the butt of Lee's SMG. "You bloody wait out there mama."

"Chucks up in here, don't it?"

"Not arf. B.O. Tremendous."

"Not a lot in here though" said Lewis kicking a bed to one side so he could see underneath it. "Keep an eye on that door Scouse just in case she comes back with a gun in her hand."

"Yeah, OK." Over in the corner Lewis pulled a bundle of rags off what he thought was a table to find that it was, in fact an old trunk. Battered and very dirty, the lid of the trunk could only be prized open with the end of Lewis's bayonet. Very slowly Lewis raised the lid then slammed it down again quickly. "Here, Scouse, just cover me a second will you? I reckon this bloody thing is big enough to hold a man. Don't want no bastard leaping out of here with a knife in his paw."

"OK" said Lee standing sideways on at the door so he could see both the area just outside the basher and his partner.

Lifting the lid slowly, Lewis suddenly let out a long slow whistle.

"Fucking shave off" he cried. "Come and get a butchers at this lot Scouse. I must be fucking seeing things" he exclaimed.

Crossing quickly to his companion, Lee was as confounded as Lewis, for there, neatly stacked in bundles was the largest amount of cash either had ever seen.

"There must be bloody millions here" beamed Lee.

"Not so loud" said Lewis shaking slightly with excitement as his mind whirled. "Let's keep this to ourselves, eh?"

"Right, but where the hell would they get this kind of dough in the middle of nowhere?"

"I don't give a shit where it came from. But I know where it's going. Get back to the door and keep a lookout while I stuff as much as I can in my ammo pouches and pockets. When I'm full, you come and do the same. Shit, looks like we've really cracked it this time my son."

"Fuckin' right. Just take the biggest denominations first, then if there's any more room left we can take some more smaller notes" said Lewis already stuffing wads of notes into his pockets.

"C'mon, Lewy, hurry up for Christ's sake. The others will be finished soon and come looking for us."

"Don't panic. I'm nearly topped up. Just got a bit more room down my trouser legs. There. OK, your turn."

"Think we should tell the rest about this lot?"

"Nah, fuck it. We could well be on the way back to Singers shortly, so there's not long to keep it stowed away from them."

"Bloody hell, we'll be able to buy bloody Singers with this lot." beamed Lee moving over to replace Lewis at the trunk.

"Just get a bloody move on"

"OK, nearly done."

Stuffing as much money as they could into every conceivable space without making their general appearance too unusual, the two emerged from the basher just in time to greet Baron who was about to come in after them and see what had kept them.

"Nothing in there. Sarge" said Lee. "You found owt?"

"Zilch. There's more pictures of the Royal Family than anything else. These buggers are more patriotic than we are. And I don't fancy eating or drinking anything from here, so I think we'll piss off and leave them to it. Bloody heaves in these bashers, too. Yours the same?"

"Yeah, chucked up something rotten. Couldn't get out of there quick enough. We did a thorough search though."

"Good lads. C'mon, let's get the rest of the gang and clear out of here." At that moment Laker appeared from out of one of the other bashers followed by a protesting local.

"What the bloody hell are you doing with that thing?" demanded Baron

"It's a banjo, Sarge."

"I can see it's a fucking banjo, but what the hell are you doing with it?"

"I'm going to while away the lonely hours learning to play it."

"And drive us all crackers in the process? No chance. Put it back. We're not here to nick stuff so if anyone else has got that in mind, forget it."

"But Sarge" protested Laker "Just think, we could have some Rudyard accompanied by music."

"No. Lakes, no. Put the bugger back."

"Now."

"Christ, can you imagine the bloody row he'd make?" said Luther.

"Perish the thought."

"Come on then lads, let's go."

"Another mission successfully completed, squad" grinned Mackay.

"You can say that again" Lee muttered to Lewis.

"Where the hell are we going to stow this lot then, Lewy?"

"It'll have to be in our packs for now. Line the bottom of them with a piece of cardboard and slide the dough underneath. Sort of a false bottom, like."

"Yeah, that'll do for the time being. How much do you reckon we've got between us?"

"Dunno. Wait until tonight and we'll try and slip out and count the bastard. Must be a few grand though. We'll have a bloody good time back in Singers on it though.

"How will we get it back to UK?"

"Buggered if I know. Probably have to exchange it at a bank in Singers and get it transferred to Blighty into an account."

"I haven't got an account, have you?"

"No. Maybe we can start one from Singers."

"Main thing is that we've cracked it at last. What're you going to do with yours?"

"Depends just how much it is. If it's thousands, and I reckon it has to be, the first thing is a bloody good weekend in the Raffles with the most expensive whore I can find and all the trimmings. Then the smartest tailor in town, buy some 'rabbits' for the family back in UK, like radios and Hi-Fi sets, and piss up the rest. What about you?"

133

"Basically the same, but instead of staying in UK I'll have a few days there then hop on a plane to the Caribbean or Bermuda or someplace like that. Somewhere that's got loads of rampant white trash just waiting for a rich bastard like me to come along and do them a favour. Let's face it, when are we ever going to get a draft to places like that so we might as well see them while we can, eh?"

"Dead right. We could go together, eh? If we get a repat on the same flight, which is bleedin' unlikely with this mob, we can have a good piss up in Smoke and piss off to Utopia after a quick visit home."

"Where the bloody hell's Utopia? Is it in the Caribbean somewhere?"

"Not exactly, but we'll find something like it there. In the meantime we'd better make sure the packs don't leave our sight for a minute. Don't trust no bastard, though we should be OK while it's just the platoon together. Let's hope we stay that way until we get back to Singers. About time we got some sort of date, Surely our bloody reliefs must be out here now or in Singers getting acclimatised, at least, so it can't be too long now."

"I reckon the bastards will keep us here as long as they can just to keep the numbers up while they start shifting different units and the bloody pongos around the world to get as many troops as they can out here."

"The eternal optimist, you are."

"Well, now we're in the money you have to plan a little bit, eh? The quicker we get out of here and back to Sembawang the better. Less time to cart it around or get it nicked by some bastard."

"True."

"C'mon, stow it away while no bastard's around."

"Shit, there must be a million in here."

"Not quite that much, but enough to keep us two in booze and whores for the odd weekend" laughed Lewis.

"How much do you make it then?" asked lee as the pair sat in the glow of a candle counting the money outside the station while the others were dozing.

"I've got ninety thousand here. And you?"

"Over a hundred thousand smackerroos, buddy."

"Fucking hell. I didn't think there'd be that much. Christ, we've really cracked it this time, Lewy. Can't wait to get out of this hole and back to Singers, now. The time's really going to drag now, eh?"

"Lee, Lewis, Moran got a job for you three. Report to Baron up at the Headquarters at the school on the double." said Mackay on replacing the head set of the Field Telephone in the station. "You're going for a little ride in a chopper."

"Shit. Where to?"

"Brunei. There's a couple of prisoners there to be picked up and brought back here. Apparently they've got some gen for us and are going to take us to a kampong where there's definitely some action going on."

"Why us?" protested Lewis. "Can't some other bugger go?"

"Baron specially selected you. Thought it might take your minds of repat for a while."

"If only he knew. Oh, well, come on Scouse the Louse, let's go. Look after the gear you lot while we are away. I don't trust these bloody Rangers as far as I can throw them."

"Makes a bit of a change I suppose" moaned Moran.

"One we could do without right now."

"Why's that then?"

"Doesn't matter."

"You bastards have got it made here, alright" Lewis ribbed a group of marines from the unit Headquarters Company as they arrived at the school in Brunei which was being used as the centre for interrogation and from where they were to collect the prisoners they were to escort back to Trusan.

Sooner be out in the bloody ulu with you lot than stuck here on guard duties all the time with the top brass up our arses every five minutes."

"Oh yeah? It's really great floggin' ourselves to death every day on patrols and ambushes and searches, never knowing when you're going to get your head blown off by some bastard lying in wait for you."

"The next time you lot from Support Company flog yourselves to death will be the first. Especially the MMGs. If I know the Baron, you sods will be the most organised platoon in the whole unit. I expect you've got a bloody knocking shop and restaurant in the middle of the bloody ulu and making a fortune."

"You must be bloody joking. It's bloody grim where we are. We can't just walk into a shower when we feel like it" lied Lee. "And we never know where the next mouthful of grub's coming from either." "Probably" added Lewis "because you buggers back here are flogging all the stuff to the rebels round the town before it even gets near us."

Sensing that there was a chance things could become very heated at any moment, Lee suggested that it be a good idea if they got a shower while they were waiting for the prisoners and something to eat if they could. Lewis was more concerned with getting some information on their repat to UK so, saying he would catch them up in a minute, turned towards the Headquarters offices.

"Check on my date too, Lewy" called Lee.

"As if I wouldn't. See you in the showers. Don't drop your soap while Moran's around." He laughed.

"Arseoles" retorted Moran.

"Correct."

"You ain't going to believe this Scouser."

"Oh shit, now what?"

"We're both booked on the same flight back to UK on March 18th. That's only six weeks away, so knock off a week or so for leaving routine back in Singers and a couple of days here in Headquarters and I make it we've just got about four weeks at the most left in this hell hole. Great, eh?"

"Shit hot. The bloody sooner the better. Is that gen?"

"Straight from the horse's mouth. Well, from the gob of that little weed Dixon in Drafting and Movements anyway, and it's more than his life's worth to bullshit me after I thumped him for fucking up our leave dates in Peneng that time."

"Thank Christ for that. Now we can plan a few runs ashore, eh?"

"Too right. First thing's a bloody great T-Bone with all the trimmings and a good piss up in the Spotlight."

"Then a good bagoff down town" added Lewis.

"Why don't' you two shit in it" said Moran.

"Never mind, Moran, your turn will come. How long to do now, is it?"

"Ten months."

"Wish I had ten months to do, don't you Lewy?"

"Yeah, especially in Bloody Borneo."

"Belt up you bastards. Come on, let's get some nosh over the galley before we have to piss off with this rebel bastard."

"Two of them ain't it?"

"Oh yeah."

"Don't suppose the bastards have been in a chopper before, so I expect they're crapping themselves."

"Perhaps we could throw them out halfway there?"

"That would please fucking Robbo no end."

"Yeah, but then we could come back and get some more and have another nosh and maybe a night here and a few bevvies."

"Do you think Headquarters have got a bleedin' box full of them or something?"

"Suppose not really."

"These two are in your charge until you get back to Trusan, Lewis. They've been 'questioned' for the last three days and the information gleaned from them is in this envelope. Give it and them to Lieutenant Robson on your return. Is that clear?"

"As a bell, sir" replied Lewis to the Intelligence Captain, a large brawny man whom Lewis felt sure enjoyed every minute of 'questioning' prisoners. Judging by the state of the two unfortunates now handed over to their care they had little doubt that both had been through a torrid time. The cut lips and the bruises around their faces told their own story. What damage had been inflicted on the not visible parts of their bodies was left to the marines' imagination, but that they had been severely beaten at some stage was clearly evident in the painful way they proceeded to shuffle out to the waiting Landover that was to take them all back to the helicopter pad.

Having strapped the two manacled prisoners into their seats Lewis, as a stick leader informed the pilot on the intercom that all was correct in the cabin of the craft and the helicopter took off for Trusan.

Through the open doorway they could see the jungle below and the maze of waterways and small islands that led from the main rivers and the coastline of Borneo itself, Later, the rivers became fewer and farther between as they approached their destination and the terrain changed to thick swamplands and small tributaries, save for the main river on which Trusan was situated.

The pilot told Lewis that they were about to start their descent and the chopper eased down just about tree level as they saw the landing pad on the field just behind the school. Slowly the helicopter was manoeuvred into a position right above the bright orange and green parachute silks that marked the landing zone and gently landed by the pilot.

A second later the green light signal indicated that they were free to disembark. Signalling Moran to get out first with the mailbag they had brought with them, Lewis and Lee proceeded to un-strap each rebel in turn and point them out of the cabin towards Robson waiting at the edge of the airstrip. Uneasy still after what was their first encounter with such a loud air machine, the rebels were reluctant to be pushed out of the door, unsure of the reception that waited for them. The first rebel, however, decided that he'd had enough of the machine and leapt out of the cabin door and rushed towards the waiting group.

He never reached them. Running in an upright position he had not gone five paces before the swirling blades decapitated him. Blood gushed out of the neck of the body high into the air and sprayed the green sward brilliant red.

Immediately Lewis grabbed the other rebel and held him in the cabin while Lee got on the intercom and told the pilot to cut the motor before they would disembark with the other rebel. Horrified at the sight of his former comrade the remaining rebel shook with fear and clung to Lewis like a limpet at the entrance to the chopper. Now the blades had stopped and the noise cut out completely.

"Didn't anyone show you how to leave a chopper?"

"No Johnny. Nobody show." the still trembling rebel replied.

"He should have ducked."

"Fucking good Intelligence section we've got, eh?" said Lewis.

Lewis then disembarked with the rebel and jogged past the bodily remains of the other man which was hurriedly being covered with parachute silk.

A furious Robson was waiting for them.

"What the hell happened Lewis?"

"He didn't duck low enough and the blades got him, sir."

"I saw that. Didn't you instruct him how to disembark from a damn helicopter?"

"He must've seen Moran get away from the chopper ducking his head, mustn't he?"

"Don't you realise these people have never seen helicopters before let alone go up in one" barked Robson.

"Well, this one tells me that no-one in our wonderful bloody Intelligence Section bothered to tell them either, so if there's any blame for this it lies with them as far as I'm concerned. How the bloody hell was I supposed to know they hadn't been told?"

"Don't swear at me, Marine Lewis or you'll be inside quicker than that. However , there may be some truth in what you say. I shall radio a report immediately and depending on the answers to my questions I shall make a decision on just where the responsibility lied. In the meantime get back to your platoon and report to Sergeant Knight."

"Yessir."

"Don't worry Lewy, my son. Wasn't your bloody fault. They can't charge you with fuck all. The Intelligence Officer is ultimately responsible for all prisoners and their safety so it's his cock up. You probably won't hear another word about it. All be hushed up, you'll see."

"I only hope you're right, Sarge. Don't want my repat fucked up. Only about four weeks to do now."

"Didn't waste your time at Headquarters then? Drafting tell you that?"

"Yeah."

"How about you then Scouser?"

"Would you believe we're on the same flight back to UK?"

"Christ. God help the poor bloody Air Hostesses."

"They'll think it's their birthday."

"Anyway, I've got some more good news for you my ansomes."

"Makes a bloody change."

"Well, the rest of the company, led by Robbo are off on a seven day patrol with the prisoner you brought in and we are to be left here to keep the peace for a whole week all by ourselves" beamed Baron.

"Bloody hell, what's come over them? Leaving us all on our todd is asking for trouble ain't it?" said Laker.

"A week's holiday at last. I'm going to move in with that bit of stuff over the road. Where's my gear?"

"Hang fire Scouser. Nobody's moving in with anybody. We've got to keep showing the flag around here."

"I'll show that bint more than a bit of a bloody flag when I get to grips with her."

"Thought you already had?"

"OK you two, that's enough for now, plenty of time for that later. First things first. The Company move out tomorrow so between now and then let's just keep the peace and quiet. No doubt some of you are aware that the day after tomorrow is the start of the Chinese New Year, and these buggers really know how to celebrate it in style. Well, they do in Singers anyway. So we could be in for a hectic time one way or another. The first thing we've got to do is make sure they know that they're not allowed to go around letting off bloody firecrackers, or we'll think we're under attack and blow their bloody heads off. But at the same time we'll have to let them let a bit of steam off or we'll get nothing out of them at all. So we'll have to play it by ear, OK?"

"So I take it that we won't be doing sod all for a week?" asked MacKay.

"Well, we'll have a little stroll now and again just to say we did something. Nothing too hectic of course."

"Of course. Perhaps we should also give the poor bloody Rangers a day off over the festivities?"

"Yeah, might not be a bad idea. In fact we'll start tomorrow night. Half of us will do duty one night, the other half the next. Then they can take over again. Don't want to be too generous do we?" grinned Baron."

"All heart, ain't he?"

"Right now my ansomes, Lakes is duty chef, so the rest of us will clean weapons, lay the boobys and get back in time for a truly a la Laker meal, before we have an hour's letter writing, a few hands of bridge and finish up with Rudyard. Now what could be a better way to spend an evening?"

"Where do you want me to start?"

"Amazes me no bugger has blown himself up yet" said Moran.

"Plenty of time, my son. Plenty of time."

"Yessir. Thank you sir. Yes, I've got that sir. No. of course sir. Goodbye sir. Good hunting sir. See you a week from today sir. Yessir. Goodbye sir. Piss off sir. Well, that's those sods off our backs for a while. There's just the anti-tanks up at the school looking after things up there. And us. C'mon my lucky lads, time we paid a visit over the road and saw how the New Year preparations are getting on."

"Will our gear be OK here while we all go Sarge?" asked Lee.

"Unusual for you to be concerned about your gear isn't it?"

"We're going home soon. Don't want bugger all nicked before we return it to the stores, do we?"

"Of course. Should be alright here though unless the Rangers get too pissed up."

"I reckon it'd be a fair idea to let the blokes who are on duty tonight stay here for now and keep an eye on things while we're away" said Mackay.

"Yeah, you could be right at that, Jock. No, on second thoughts, let those on tonight come with us now until around midday, then they can come back and get their heads down before going on watch. So Scouser, Lewy and Lakes stay here and just keep an eye on things and clean up a bit, or write, or read some Rudyard if you want and the rest of us will relieve you around one o'clock, OK?" smiled Baron.

"Right-o-Sarge. Don't get too pissed and forget us though, will you?" asked Laker.

"How could I possibly forget you, my little Brummie friend" laughed Baron.

"Come on lads, let's get going then." The three left in the station spent the morning idly playing cards reading and writing after having tidied up the room and the kitchen and toilet and shower room. Lewis at one stage decided to sit quietly in the sun on the steps outside the room and was slowly humming to himself the song Wooden Heart which was very popular at the time, when from the house next to the station a little Malay girl appeared on the steps watching him. Only about four years old, but very beautiful, she too knew the song and proceeded to sing along with Lewis in her native tongue. Both beaming all over their faces they repeated the same song for ten minutes until, as quickly as she had appeared, she was gone, skipping over the road to one of the other buildings.

Chinese New Year

"Ere, you ought to see the spread they've laid on over at the laundry. Christ, I don't know where the bloody hell they get all the stuff from, but it's like a bloody Roman feast like you see on the pictures" burbled Moran, half staggering into the station.

"There's a bloody great table completely full of meat and fruit and rice and all sorts. The booze is flowing like water and it's a right rave up over there. Baron's half pissed already, and bloody Jock's trying to show the rebels how to do the Highland Fling, or whatever it's called. Somehow they've got hold of some real Scotch, so Jock is in his element."

"What about Ginge? Is he pissed yet?"

"He's well on the way."

"You don't look too bloody healthy either."

"I'm OK at the moment. Feel as fat as a pig, though."

"When are you lot coming back here?" asked Lee."

"Well, I've just had a good spew so I don't want any more of that lot for now. We've got three days of this don't forget, and every few minutes someone from one of the other houses comes and tries to drag us all into their place for the same nosh up. Baron says we'll have to go to every house eventually or they'll take it as an insult. Fuck knows how we'll ever make it."

"Fucking good job Robbo's not around, eh?" said Lewis.

"Shit, yeah, he'd go bleeding spare if he saw that lot over there right now."

"Any talent around?" asked Lee.

"Not a lot in that place. Must be spread out along the street somewhere. The bloody Rangers are as pissed as newts as well. They won't last much longer, either."

"Come on then lads, what are we waiting for?"

"Hang about Lakes. While I remember. Baron says we've not to set the traps tonight because the state some of these bastards are going to be in , they'll blow themselves and us to buggery. And we'll all be too pissed to set them properly, too, so best leave it for a while. It'll take us the three days of New Year to get to the end of the street, I reckon anyway, the way things are going."

"Nothing like a good piss-up" said Lee getting his shirt on.

"Yeah, let's go."

"Hang on. Give Baron this" said Moran tossing Baron's book of poems to Lewis.

"I can't believe it." exclaimed lee.

"'Fraid so. He's promised them some Western culture and he's just waiting for you to get back with this. Enjoy yourselves" said Moran sinking to the ground on his sleeping bag.

"Hey, keep an eye on our bloody gear, Moran."

"Don't panic. Piss off the lot of you and let me sleep."

"Come on then lads. I could drink the bloody Mersey dry right now."

"And I'm bleedin' starving" added Lewis.

"That's all you buggers think about, ain't it? Food and booze."

"ark at him. The next time you think of refusing anything for nothing it will be the first time."

"Go on, piss off." Entering the laundry to the cheers of an emphatically drunk Mackay, Lee, Lewis and Laker took in the scene. Spread out on a pile of cushions in one corner of the room, his arm around a quite youngish girl who was busy pouring him a drink, Baron's face broke into a grin on the arrival of his comrades.

"Come on my sons, sit down and get stuck into this little lot. Give my boys a drink somebody and some cushions to sit on"

He beckoned to the mama of the house who had already guided them to the lavishly spread table.

"Shave off. And this is just the first house. How the hell are we going to get through the others?"

"Play it off the cuff, my sons" smiled Baron. "Have a good munch and a few pints and we'll move off to the next place. This rebel next door keeps coming in and trying to drag us off so we'd better go and pay him a visit. Always come back here later, eh"

"Yeah. Where's all the talent then?"

"I think those young girls only work here, so they are probably in the other houses up the road."

"Come on then" said Lee, "let's piss off and find them."

"Hold on. Can't just piss off like that, you'll upset them. And besides, I promised them a bit of culture. Where's Rudyard? Did you bring my book?"

"Here, catch."

"Ah. Gather round my friends for the treat of your little Asiatic lives. Great white Sergeant will educate you in ten classics. Well, not all of them, but a good dose of Rudyard, second only to the Bard himself." grinned Baron.

"Here we go again....."

"We'll start off with my favourite, 'Soldier and Sailor Too' and then go on to some of the others. All sitting comfortably? Then I'll begin....."

"Just like Watch with Mother, ain't it?"

"But I ain't in the mood for watching. What say you two?" asked Lee.

"Took the words right out of my mouth" Lee agreed. "Can't sit here while there's some fanny up the road somewhere."

"We'll pop off next door sarge and keep that guy happy until you get there. Don't forget to wake Jock up before you go. Don't leave the bugger lying there all night" called Laker as the three eased their way over the prostrate figure of Mackay sprawled half across the doorway.

"What happened to the bloody Highland Fling?" grinned Lee.

"Don't you lads want to sit and listen as well?" cried Baron from the floor.

"Not just now Sarge, thanks. Not the same as when you read to us in bed" said Lee.

"I quite understand my sons. Carry on. See you in a minute."

"You piss-taking sod" Lewis chided Lee. "You'll hurt his bloody feelings.

"He's too far gone to care. Let's go." Stepping out onto the verandah they were immediately accosted by the owners of the next house and ushered into a large room, the replica of the one previous. As before, a magnificent table full of an array of fruits, meats and rice waited for them with an ample supply of beverages stacked on an adjacent table. One subtle difference was the sight of three young girls waiting to attend to them. All of similar height, they were dressed in gaily coloured sarongs of blue, red and green which accentuated their dark, shiny skin and hugged their surprisingly curvaceous figures.

"Now this is a bit more like it" Lee gleefully exclaimed. Shut the bloody door and let's get stuck into this lot.

"I could eat a dead moggie" laughed Laker.

"When couldn't you?"

"Hello darling. Been waiting patiently for my body have you?" "Well, the thrill of a lifetime will surely be yours as soon as I can throw some of this nosh and booze down" said lee sliding his arm around the prettiest of the girls.

"Don't waste any bloody time, does he?"

"Nil decorum."

"Piss off you two. We might get bombed by the bloody Indonesians at any minute. Then I'd be sitting up there playing my harp and thinking what an arseole I was for wasting time and missing out on life's little pleasures."

"Philosophical bastard, ain't he?"

"Yeah" agreed Lewis "but bloody good thinking all the same. Come on, lets' get going."

"OK, I'm convinced."

Having laid into the food and wine with great gusto to the delight of the guy and his family, the three young marines allowed 'nature to take its course' as Lee put it, and promptly led the three girls away to the back of the house without a word of protest from their parents who seemed as delighted at the prospect as the others.

Hardly had they left, when Baron's large bulk filled the doorway of the house. Through bleary, half closed eyes he tried to penetrate the darkness of the room and find his charges.

"What're you buggers up to ? Where the bloody hell are they?"

"Commandos take girls for looksee at keckchings. Say not to be disturbed at all Sergeant, sir." The old man grinned, rubbing his hands together and showing the jet black beetle stained teeth in his wizened mouth.

"Kecks o' etchings?" asked Baron swaying slightly as he leant heavily on the door frame.

"Yes Sergeant sir. That's right. In private room. You sit and wait. Plenty food and boozies. Verlly happy time at New Year."

"Brandy.

"Yessir Sergeant sir. Big brandy for big Sergeant, sir. You want nice girlie too? Me get you best girlie in whole Borneo. Very special."

"Let's have a butchers then. Go and get this gem of the Orient."

"Me go fetch, back velly now." Bowing almost to the floor, the old man scurried out.

"Hold it" Baron shouted after him. "Who's that then?" he said pointing to the plump woman sat opposite him on a cane chair,"

"That wife, Sergeant sir. Not good time girlie, you understand sir?"

"Just as bloody well" said Baron struggling to focus on her.

"Bit grotty, eh?"

"Sorry Sergeant sir. What grotty?" asked the man bowing again.

"Stop bloody bowing up and down. Making me bloody sea sick. Just run away and get me this woman, OK?"

"Me run velly fast, Sergeant sir. Come back velly soon." Sinking into a very frail looking chair, Baron reached for a plate of food on the nearby table, missed, and crashed to the floor. Rolling over he decided that it wasn't worth the effort and within seconds was snoring profusely, much to the amazement of the woman, who gingerly stepped around him on her way out of the room."

Ten minutes later, Lewis entered the room, dressed only in shorts and streaming with sweat, his hair plastered against his scalp. "Come and have a look at this lads" he called to the others.

"Bloody hell" laughed Laker. "Look at the state of that."

"Like a beached whale, ain't it?" said Lee joining them while retaining his hold on the semi nude girls.

"Stick one of those cushions under his bonce. Poor old bugger's bloody knackered." After making Baron as comfortable as they could, they once more tackled the huge amount of food and drink at their disposal.

"Could be a worse way to fight a war I guess." said Lewis stuffing the wing of a chicken into his mouth.

"Wonder what bloody Robbo and the others are up to?"

"I don't know and I don't give a fuck anyway" answered Lee.

"Talking of which, where the hell did you find that one?" gasped Lee as the old man returned with the most beautiful Chinese girl any of them had seen in a long time.

"Shit shoot Lieutenant. Who does she belong to?" said Lewis admiring the long, jet black hair, hour-glass figure and beautiful face of the girl.

"This very special girl for Sergeant sir. Why him asleep?" asked the guy.

"Sergeant having a little half hour's kip. I must take over all duties and responsibilities" said Lee sidling over to the girl and placing an arm around her bare shoulders.

"Don't know where he gets the bloody stamina from" moaned Laker.

"Practice."

"That figures. Mind you, that one is something else. Any more like her about?" Lewis enquired hopefully.

"This velly special girl. Only one in whole of Borneo so beautiful" replied the man.

"You can say that again" breathed Lee, staring into the sleek almond shaped eyes of the girl. Her long swan-like neck gave way to the cleavage between her full breasts which strained against the deep purple material of the sarong she was wearing as Lee's hands eased down to her right breast and stroked it sensuously.

"Oh Christ, he's in love again."

"I can't say I blame him" drooled Laker. "I'll console myself with the thought that she's probably got black syph and crabs and anything else that's going, so I'm better off without her."

"See you fellas later" said Lee refilling two glasses and guiding the girl back into the room they had previously used. "Don't wait up for me, I may be detained for some time" he called over his shoulder, winking.

"Baron, my old son, you don't know what you missed" said Lewis looking down at the sleeping Sergeant. "C'mon Lakes, lets' try and get him back to the station and his pit. He'll be more comfortable there."

"Yeah, then we can come back for more."

"Haven't you had enough?"

"Such a pity to waste all that food and booze."

"It'll be dark in a couple of hours, so if you want to come back we'd better get a move on. Help me get him upright. Come Sarge, ups a daisy. Shit, it's like trying to raise the bloody Titanic."

"We'll never carry him that far by ourselves, Lewy. I'll nip over to the station and get a couple of the lads to give us a hand. Hang on."

Shortly , Moran and Linden returned with Laker. "Shave off, what happened to him?" exclaimed Moran.

"He's OK. Just needs a hand getting back, that's all. Come on lads; two-six, heave." With each of the marines taking an arm or a leg, Baron was carted unceremoniously back to the station.

"Chuck him on his sleeping bag and throw one over him. He'll sleep for ages yet."

"Bet he' ll have one hell of a hangover in the morning."

"Our leader. What a fuckin' state to get into."

"Ere, talking of bloody leaders" exclaimed Moran,

"Where the bloody hell's the other one?"

"Who?"

"Bloody Jock, of course."

"Christ, last I saw of him, he was asleep in the laundry. S'pose he's still there. Come on Lakes, we'd better check he's alright." Quickly trotting over to the laundry across the road the two marines entered the doorway of the building only to be halted in their tracks by the sight before them. There on the table in the centre of the room, nude from the waist downwards, bent double touching his toes and encouraging the local inhabitants to throw their drinks as far as they could up his backside was RM179745 Corporal Mackay J.A in the final throes of the well known Royal Marine party piece *This Old Hat of Mine.*

"Come on Jimmy, throw the bloody stuff up my arse or you'll never be a bloody Royal Marine" shouted Mackay.

"Aye, an' you hen. What're you waiting for lassie?"

"Throw it, girl" called Laker."

"Drown the bugger" laughed Moran."

Hearing his comrades' encouragement, Mackay yelled
"Show these sods what it's all about, lads. Come on."
"Right-O you haggis waffling bastard" shouted Laker,
"Stand by to stand by."

With that they both grabbed one of the many glasses laying around and emptied the contents in the prescribed manner, encouraging their astounded hosts to follow suit, which they finally did with such gusto and hilarity that the NCO slipped on the wet table and crashed to the floor. None the worse for the fall, Mackay recovered his stance and grabbed one of the girls present, hoisted her onto the table and stood clapping as he encouraged her to copy his act. All too willing to oblige, the girl proceeded to mimic Mackay's act and shortly received the final accolade, to the resounding cheers of all.

"Fuck me, she's a rough looking bitch. Must be the local horse. Every bugger must be riding that."
"Slack as a yak" agreed Laker.
"Yeah. What's she up to now then?"

The girl, plump, with large drooping breasts and huge black nipples was now performing her own act to the cheers and encouragement of the locals and Mackay especially who clapped and yelled at the top of his voice. Now, completely nude, she placed a bottle in the centre of the table and proceeded to sway, legs astride over it. Her fat, trembling thighs wobbled as she moved snake fashion round the table slowly lowering her body towards the neck of the bottle. Before the marines' astonished gaze she finally squatted over the bottle as the neck entered her vagina. Straightening, she slowly rose to an upright position lifting the bottle with her to the great cheers of the locals and Mackay.

"Fucking shave off, lads. Magic, eh?" Mackay enthralled.
"Different, that's for sure" agreed Laker.
"Get her to do it again, Jock" said Moran.
"Yeah , go on" urged Laker.
"Right you are lads. Hey, hen, again, again."

But the woman was reluctant to perform again until Moran suggested that she could earn herself a dollar for her efforts if she could pickup in the same fashion, a fifty cent coin balanced on the top of the neck of the bottle.

The offer was too good for the woman to resist and amid the cheers she clambered back onto the table , replacing the bottle in the centre of it." Pick it up without dropping it and we'll give you a dollar each" cried MacKay above the now growing crowd squeezing into the room. Lewis and Linden had also come across the street on hearing the cheers to investigate.

"What's going on?" asked Lewis.

Moran placed the fifty cent coin on top of the bottle and stood back and clapped and cheered with the crowd.

"OK Johnny marines, me try" the woman called above the hullabaloo, as she started to girate, thoroughly enjoying her new found fame and popularity.

"Quick, gather round lads and give me a match" Moran whispered to his pals.

"What are you up to now?" asked Laker.

"Just give me a match and another fifty cent coin somebody, quickly." A coin and matches were produced and as the woman cavorted around the table Moran held the coin between the folds of his trousers with one hand and held a match to it with the other.

"Shit, that's hot" he whispered.

"You bastard."

"Watch this lads." he said grinning.

Waiting until the woman neared the final stages of her act and had her large rear staring them virtually in their faces as she circled for the last time before attempting to pick up the coin, Moran deftly , reached between her legs, and exchanged the coins. So enjoying the new acclaim was she that she did not notice at all and finally, facing the marines she started to lower herself the last few inches to the bottle neck and the coin.

"Wait for it lads." Intoxicated with her new found fame and concentrating so hard was she that it took a second or two for her to realise that what she had between her legs was not what she expected. Her facial expression changed from a broad grin of confidence to pain in one instant as she literally 'took off' and crashed to the floor to the roars of the marines and the locals who, though not quite sure what had happened relished the sight of her sprawled in agony on the ground trying desperately to remove the coin from inside her.

"Time to go, methinks" laughed Moran.

"I agree. She's doing her fuckin' nut over there."

"Wouldn't you with a hot fifty up your fanny?"

"Reckon I would at that."

"Fucking funny though. haven't laughed so much since granny caught her tit in the mangle" grinned Laker.

"Here, look at Jock pouring beer over her parts. Thinks he's in the fucking Fire Brigade."

"Let's leave him to it, he'll be alright for awhile. Probably crawl though her before he fucks off, anyway."

"I wouldn't touch that with yours" replied Lewis.

"Better tell him we're off. It'll be dark soon and we can't have him wandering around all over the place."

"You lads go back, I'll hang on for him. And don't forget bloody Scouse, either. He's' shafting that bird next door, so someone check on him, too."

"Fuck my old sea boots, my bloody head's killing me. Where's the first aid kit and the codine?" growled Baron emerging from his sleeping bag the next morning.

"Here" said Luther. Drink this with them" handing Baron a steaming mug of tea and two tablets.

"Thanks Ginge. Bloody hell, I feel lousy. Where's everyone else, are they all as knackered too?"

"All present and correct and just about as hung-over as you. Nothing exciting happened in the night, though the locals were pissing it up all the way through. No problems though. Fucking good job we didn't lay the traps I reckon. There'd be bodies all over the show all night."

"What happened to me then? The last thing I remember was waiting for some guy to bring me a bit of stuff from somewhere or other. Then blank."

"You flaked out."

"Yeah. Don't worry about it though" said Lee. "She wasn't up to much."

"Not many, Benny."

"Oh yea, Sarge. There's been two guys in here for you this morning. They want to have a bloody procession or something through the street this afternoon, so I told them to come back and see you later."

"OK. What's happened to the Rangers?"

"Two have got their heads down and the other is sat in the office trying to write a report or something like that. They're all as fucked as we are."

"What's on the me an' you for today then Sarge?" asked Lewis.

"First get a bloody shower and wake up properly. Then I'll sort out this procession or whatever it is. Then just play it off the cuff, my sons, play it off the cuff. Oh my bleedin' head."

"Give us they tablets Sarge" drawled Mackay, his long nose appearing over the top of the next sleeping bag. "Tea, some bugger, quick, before I die."

"Fuck me, he's in a worse state then I am" said Baron.

"Don't worry. Even though our great leaders have been out of action, we have carried on the war without loss" Luther dramatically called from the doorway.

"Bollicks."

"Open that bloody door Ginger, for Chrissake. It bloody hustles in here. And you sods can get this pad cleaned up a bit while I get organised" ordered Baron.

An hour later, in much better heart Baron received the deputation from the town led, as it happened by the very guy who had so generously entertained them the previous day. Baron, therefore felt obliged to permit a small parade along the street that late afternoon and sent the representatives away rejoicing. The parade turned out to be a gay, colourful procession of imitation dragons, tigers and long floats of men and women under huge costumes of silken animals who wound their way in and out of every house, apparently as a sign that the devils were not in the buildings and it was safe to live there for the year. The whole parade danced its way along the street to the accompaniment of a collection of strange musical instruments the marines had never seen before. Flutes carved from bamboo and whistles and drums and what turned out to be bones created a loud, not unattractive throng of noise for the watching visitors and the crowd that lined the street.

"Like Liverpool scoring the winner in the bloody Cup Final ain't it?" said Lee.

"Yeah. Quite something when you realise we're in the middle of the bloody ulu."

"Beats me how they manage to get all this gear out here" remarked Moran swigging from a bottle of beer.

"It's probably handed down through the ages and they just keep replacing the worn parts as necessary" said Mackay.

"What like Scouse's chopper?" laughed Lewis.

"Watch it, my son."

"I would if I could find it."

"Ha bloody ha."

"Looks like it's just about over now Sarge" said Laker. "And this guy here keeps asking us to go to his house, no doubt for another piss-up. I'm fucked though, don't know about you lot?"

"We'll have to go" said Baron.

"We can't leave any bugger out or they'll get bloody upset. How many more places are there we haven't been in yet?"

"About five I make it" replied Mackay.

"Bloody hell, we'll never do it. And there's tomorrow to go yet."

"Tell you what we'll do. Split into two groups and do two places each and leave the final one for tomorrow. We'll finish up with a good session in the last house, all together, like. What say Jock? A good idea?"

"Yeah, I reckon that'd be best. But we must try and stay a bit more sober than yesterday. We can't have Robbo coming back unexpected and uninvited and catching us looking like bloody death, eh?" agreed Mackay.

"True. So you take Moran and Ginger and I'll look after the rest."

"Who's going to look after who?" asked Laker.

"Will our gear be OK if we're all out at the same time?" queried Lee.

"I don't know why you two are so bloody worried about your gear all the time. It'll be OK with the Rangers on watch. I promised them another day off if they looked after things today. But we'll pop back every now and then to keep a check in case they all get pissed up again." Sneaking a quick look at Lee, Lewis vowed to nip back on his own and make sure their kit was alright.

"C'mon.. lets stuff our faces while we can. Bloody Robbo will soon be giving us some stick again. Which reminds me, we'd better do a smally patrol before he gets back. Perhaps a little stroll out to that farm again."

"Yeah, why not Sarge? We could use the exercise after this little lot."

"Gone all Corps pissed all of a sudden haven't we?"

"Well, we are Britain's bloody commandos; the lean, mean fighting machines....." laughed Laker.

"The bloody booze has gone to his head."

"Come on, I'm hungry."

"You're always bloody hungry. how does that poor woman put up with you?"

"'Cos I'm essence...." joked Baron, puckering his fat lips.

"Must cost a fortune what with the kids and all."

"Yeah, but don't forget all that Living Overseas Allowance he gets every week."

"Have you two quite finished discussing my financial plight?" asked Baron.

Moving out to the end of the street to the last five houses, the two groups parted and entered their respective places of entertainment.

Both enjoyed their fill of food and drink before moving to the next place where more drink was consumed. Only a disappointed Lee, who failed to find the girl he had encountered the previous day, remained fairly sober and it was he who nipped back to the station to check on their gear. Finding everything in order, he returned to the house they had been in the day before and questioned the guy on the whereabouts of the girl. But to his further dismay, the guy told him that she had returned to her father's house way up the river and was not expected back again in the near future.

Returning to his comrades, Lee indicated to Lewis that all was well with their gear and then proceeded to drown his disappointment in the usual manner.

"I don't like keep leaving that loot around when we're not about"

154

said Lewis. I reckon we should bury it somewhere.

"Nah, it'll be OK where it is. Bloody funny actually. We've got a police guard on stolen property if you look at it that way."

"I don't trust bloody cops at the best of times."

"Me neither, but we ain't got a lot of choice have we?"

"Come on, let's sink a few and then get our heads down. I'm quite knackered."

"Thank Christ tomorrow is the last day of the New Year. The pace is killing me, too." As dusk fell the marines returned to their station and allowed the Rangers to go and celebrate.

On the last day of the festivities the last house in the village laid on a fantastic spread for everyone in the street. Tables laden with all manner of delicacies spilled onto the road as the locals and the marines feasted to the accompaniment of the local musicians with their pipes and drums and whistles.

"Not quite the bloody Massed Bands is it? But they're not too bad all the same" said Lee emptying yet another glass of wine.

"Look at bloody Jock up the end of the street" called Laker pointing to the tall Scotsman who had somehow collected all the children of the village together and placed them in single file behind him as he led them around the street playing on his chanter.

"Looks like the fucking Pied Piper, don't he?"

"The blind following the bloody blind. Only he's blind drunk" laughed Baron.

"Go on my son."

"Look at the Rangers" shouted Linden. "They're all as pissed as arseoles again" he said pointing to them, staggering between the building.

"In unison, Lee and Lewis looked at each other."

"Who the fuck is looking after the station" yelled Lee quickly getting to his feet.

"Who fucking cares?" burbled Laker.

"I fucking do. My gear's in there." Lee replied running off towards the billet.

"What the fuck's up with him?" said Baron.

"He's OK. Probably the booze has gone to his head" answered Lewis.

"I'll go and check him. I've had enough, as it is. Knackered."

"Wonders will never cease. Never thought I'd see the day when you two left a piss up early." said Baron.

"Getting bloody old, aren't we?" called Lewis over his shoulder.

"Is it all there?"

"Yeah. And I've found a loose panel in the shower that will fit this lot perfectly. We can slide it in there and forget it until we piss off. No bugger will think of looking for anything there. OK?" asked Lee.

"Let's have a look first. Get the stuff."

"There, fits like a fucking glove. Great." Sliding the plastic bags into position in the niche behind the shower taps and replacing the tiles, the two marines were well pleased with the safety of their treasure.

"How much longer is this bloody rain going on for Jimmy?" Mackay asked one of the Rangers.

"Usually only three days at a time sir. Stop tomorrow perhaps."

"Bloody better or we'll be flooded out. That river's getting too bloody high for my liking."

For two days the heavens had opened and torrential monsoon rains had pounded the tiny village of Trusan. Streams of water ran down the street carrying mulch and slush from the higher ground right through the village. Marines and civilians alike had been confined to their dwelling places except for those who had animals tended in the temporary shelters which were constructed for such emergencies. They had to go and feed the animals daily, but no-one else was to be seen moving around the village at all.

Baron had decided that this was an ideal time for the rebels to be on the move so the trip flares and grenades had once more been installed as a precaution and Lee and Lewis had just returned from the morning trip to dis-arm them.

"Hey Sarge" called Lewis from outside the billet. Opening the door Baron saw a drenched Lewis and Lee with a native of the village between them.

"What's up?"

"This guy's in a panic 'cos his one and only cow has been swept into the river out there, look, and he can't get the bastard out. Wants us to go out in the dugout and get it for him. Don't know how long it's gonna stay stuck up against that tree trunk out there. Probably drown by the time we get near it"

"Maybe. Right lads, Lee and Lewis are already like drowned rats, so they can stay wet. One volunteer to help me and them get the bugger out? Good lad Lakes. Knew I could rely on you."

"Fucking thanks, Sarge." moaned Laker.

"We need a big strong lad like you. Come on, let's go." Taking the guy and a length of rope with them, the marines slid their way down to the edge of the river which was now in full flow and into the dugout. Paddling hard, they headed towards the large tree that had been washed down from upstream and jammed in the water directly opposite the station. Luckily for the unfortunate cow it had been swept straight into the path of the tree and was now jammed up against it while the torrid waters raced by.

"Get a line around its neck" Baron yelled from the rear of the boat.

"And then tie it to the end of the boat."

"Keep bloody paddling hard lads or we'll be washed down the stream too" shouted Lee. Taxing all their individual strength to hold the boat on a steady course against the fierce current, the Marines managed to secure a line around the animal's neck and attached the other end to the front of the boat. Through the pouring rain Baron yelled encouragement to his men as they struggled to the shore, towing the cow behind . The guy was now bent over the back of the craft attempting to hold his animal's head out of the water. A sudden swell almost took him overboard until Lee grabbed him and hauled him back. Eventually, their sweat mingled with the rain on their soaking , sweating and steaming bodies, the band managed to get the distraught animal ashore to the overwhelming thanks of the bedraggled guy who happily led his heaving animal away.

"That's our good deed for the day over lads" called Baron as they secured the dugout considerably higher up the bank.

"Well done my ansomes."

"I thought the bastard had had it though" said Lewis.

"Never mind the bloody cow, I thought the guy had shit it until Scouse grabbed him."

"Poor little bastard. Probably all he's got in life." said Baron.

"Plenty of hot char ready when you are lads" called Mackay from the doorway of the station.

"Good lad Jock. Be with you right now".

"Bloody water's got into the billet now Sarge through a crack in the wall of the shower. 'Shored it up as best we could, but I reckon we might have to move out if it goes on raining much longer." Lee and Lewis looked at each other.

"Hole in the shower?" asked Lewis.

"Yeah. Nothing much, but the water started pissing through it. Better keep an eye on it though."

"Come on Scouse, let's see if we can't do something about it, what with your technical knowledge of building and plastering.

"Or getting plastered, more like it."

"Balls. OK, let's go and have a shuffty." And the two, after stripping off their wet clothes down to their underpants filtered into the station as casually as they could.

"That's OK" whispered Lee. "The hole is below the stuff, so it won't run into it."

"Better check it regularly. Once one part starts falling apart, there's always another to follow"

"Don't worry, it'll be alright."

"Oh Christ, he's back. Got to go up for an O Group. Won't be long. Keep the kettle boiling. Come on Moran, let's go."

"Better get our heads down early tonight lads. Robbo and the rest of the Company are picking us up at bloody 3a.m. on the way to a cordon and search tomorrow morning. We'd better do the guard tonight just in case the bugger tries something on. No traps out tonight. We won't have time to dismantle them before dawn."

"Looks like the holidays are over Sarge."

"Yeah, but I also heard a buzz this may be our last little effort in Trusan. Sigs reckons we're on the move again soon. Up nearer to Brunei. Anyway, we'll see. For now let's get some grub on and a few hands in before an early night."

"Nearer Brunei, eh?" said Lee."

"Sounds a bit promising. I like it." agreed Lewis.

"No buzzes on you two getting back to Singers, so don't get too bloody excited." said Baron.

"You'll bloody miss us when we go Sarge won't you?"

"Like a hole in the fucking head. Now give Lakes a hand in the galley before he fucks the lot up while I sort out a duty guard list for tonight."

"What the fuck.......? What's all the fucking banging? Get the light on somebody. Oh no. Shit, it's bloody Robbo and his gang. Get rigged. What's the time? Who's on watch? Bloody Lakes. I'll hang from him." said Baron in several breaths as he struggled to get out of his sleeping bag.

"Sergeant Knight, get up at once. Where are your men? Who is supposed to be on watch? Why aren't you ready for the patrol?" stammered Robson.

"Just coming sir. Slight hitch in communications. Sir. Almost ready. With you in a jiffy." And in a lower tone

"Move your arses lads for fuck's sake."

Pushing the door open Robbo took in the scene.

"Nice of you to join us Sergeant. So sorry to have disturbed you at this unearthly hour. Do extend my apologies to your men."

"That's alright sir. We've been doing a lot of patrols while you've been away so we're used to getting up a bit...."

"Shut up Sergeant or you won't be one. Get your men fell in outside on the end of the patrol ready to move off. I'll deal with this rabble you call a platoon later."

"Yessir. You heard the officer lads. Move it."

"Sorry Sarge" a breathless Laker reported. "Must've nodded off. Never heard a thing until Robbo started banging on the bloody door. The sod must've crept up to try and catch us on purpose."

"Bloody succeeded didn't he?"

"Rhodesian git" offered Linden."

The cordon and search consisted of the whole patrol surrounding the kampong two miles away to the east and lying in wait until dawn in the hope that there would be some movement involving rebels. However, this time again the exercise proved fruitless, the only movement being that of a family of wild boar which passed close to Laker and Moran causing them to hastily change positions thereby giving away the presence of the patrol to the occupants of the village who shortly afterwards came out to stand and stare at Robbo and his signaller, much to their annoyance and embarrassment.

To Sundar

Two days later the Company was assembled on the helicopter strip above the village of Trusan ready for airlifting to their new location. It was with decidedly mixed feelings that the MMG platoon left the village. While not an island paradise it had been comfortable and very hospitable. For a theatre of war there were many less palatable places to be and the friendliness of the people and their generosity would, they felt take some beating.

But a move in any direction towards Brunei was a step nearer repat for Lee and Lewis and with their own private treasure chest safely stowed in their gear they looked forward to the next location.

A large clearing at the edge of the river with just two huts positioned at right angles to it, surrounded by thick jungle was Sundar. Nothing else. From the air they saw that nowhere in the near vicinity was there any sign of habitation and , slightly dejected they landed and were divided into the two huts, the MMG's and the AEs sharing one while Robbo, and his HQ staff shared with the Mortars.

Having set up good communications with Commando Headquarters in Brunei it was established at the evening's O Group that their task was to patrol the surrounding jungle but more importantly the river and the small tributaries leading from it into the swamps. Their job was to move quickly into any area where Headquarters' received information that there was troop movement and to set up static ambushes on the rivers.

On their second day at Sundar the MMG platoon was ordered to set up an ambush two miles from the camp at the intersection of the three rivers. They were to stay for 48 hours and report on the movements on the rivers over the radio to Headquarters direct, from where decisions would be made on whether to intercept the traffic or let it pass for further observation farther up river. Moving out from Sundar at the crack of dawn, the platoon in two large dugouts headed for their position only too glad to break the monotony of the camp and the daily exercise programmes Robson had devised for them.

Their hideaway proved to be a long bamboo and reed construction on stilts at the water's edge. Half of the construction had been allowed to rot away completely leaving just the frame but the remaining room was sufficient for the platoon to be accommodated in reasonable comfort. Having secured the dugouts the marines scampered up the rickety framework into the basher and unloaded their minimal supplies, at the completion of which they were surprised by two impertinent monkeys who cheekily scampered into the room by means of the window and promptly snatched two packets of their precious sugar supply before retreating back through the window.

Lewis, detailed by Baron for the first watch said

"Don't worry Sarge, I'll get the buggers if they come around again. Doubt if they will now that we've scared them off though."

"I'll leave that in your tender care then my son, but keep a good eye on the river just in case some bugger turns up, eh?" smiled Baron.

"Yeah, OK."

"Shake me when it's nosh time or a bit of fanny floats by" called Lee from a corner.

"Break out the bromide for fuck's sake, he's off again."

"That's what they had in the war weren't it?" asked Laker.

"That's what they should've given your old man, Lakes. Saved us a load of bother, that's for sure."

"Bollicks and good night."

"I'll shake you in two hours Lakes. OK?"

"Fucking have to be won't it?"

For over an hour Lewis sat patiently watching the river and the surrounding area of any activity. Lonely watches like this were always a time for contemplation and thoughts of home. Lewis considered the position and his personal situation and thought that he was in rather a fortunate phase of his young life. With just a couple of weeks hopefully until he was repatriated he had had a good commission on the whole. He'd seen a lot of things and places, had his share of the most beautiful women in the world he considered, been highly successful in the football world and gained celebrity status in the unit, and had come through a terrifying ordeal so far unscathed. Then as a bonus he and Lee were in possession of a huge amount of cash which could secure their futures for life. Not bad for a twenty year old, he mused. Life could indeed be a lot worse.

The river was calm and peaceful except for the normal jungle noises and the movements of the large crane-like birds that landed occasionally on the water or waded along the shore line pecking at the mud where literally hundreds of mud-hoppers provided them with an abundant supply of nutrition.

Suddenly a slight movement to his right caught Lewis's attention. Turning his head very slowly he could just make out something moving at the end of the basher by the window. Slipping the safety catch off his sub machine gun he slowly eased himself upright and started to creep towards the window. After only two paces he was aware of the cause of the movement. Monkeys. Two of them.

Raising his gun he waited until both creatures emerged from the window and started to make their escape from down the single pole that led from the basher to the shore, clasping their ill-begotten sugar packets in their small human-like hands. With devastating accuracy Lewis placed two bullets into the heads of the monkeys before they even knew that he was there.

"Got the little bastards." Lewis, in the process of eliminating the theft of their supplies, had at the same time caused a minor riot within the sleeping quarters of the basher. After an hour of comparative silence, the marines had, to a man, slipped into a deep slumber. However, with their minds and bodies programmed to react immediately to an emergency, the sound of the firing so close to them made them react instantly. Fearing that they were under enemy attack their priority was to evacuate the basher immediately, and to this end Mackay, Luther and Moran all tried to emerge from the doorway at the same time with the result that the whole wall collapsed under their combined weight, throwing them all to the floor. Laker had attempted to climb out of the back window, but landed on a fragile strip of rotten bamboo that gave way under his weight, plummeting him downwards so that he now sat waist deep in water and mud on the shore-line.

Lee fired two shots into the cloudless sky narrowly missing a passing heron and Baron was still trying to find one of his jungle boots.

Above all the chaos Lewis repeatedly yelled that it all was a mistake and eventually got his message through.

"You fucking idiot. What the bleeding hell do you think you're on?" yelled Mackay.

"I told you I was going to take care of those bloody monkeys didn't I?"

"Yeah, that's right. So you did. But we were all asleep in there. Could've been the whole Indonesian army out there for all we knew."

"How the fuck was I to know you were all asleep? What am I supposed to be, a bleeding clairvoyant?"

"OK you two, cut it out. Panic over. Let's get the side of the basher fixed up somehow and get some nosh on the go before it gets dark."

"Never mind the bloody nosh" came the voice from below them "How about you bastards getting me back up there?" yelled Laker.

"Jesus, look at the state of that" grinned Linden leaning out the back window.

"You can't come back up here in that state Lakes. You'll stink the bloody place out. Go and have a swim in the river and get all that shit off you."

"If you think I'm swimming in that with all the bloody sea snakes and weirdies floating about in there, you're fucking mistaken."

"There's an old canvas bucket in the back. Top it up and swill him down when he gets back up. Take him to the far end too." said Baron.

"Trust bloody Lakes to end up in the oggin. Must've been a racing certainty that he'd be the one to get wet" laughed Lee.

"I bet he fucking hustles."

"Right lads, check weapons before it's dark and I'll make out the duties for tonight" said Baron once more relaxing on the floor. For the duration of their stay they made no contact at all with any river traffic and thus reporting to Headquarters, were instructed to return to Sundar. However, en route they were ordered to make a series of incursions into the swamps in the hope of running across some activity amongst the enemy.

Gathering their meagre supplies and kit together the marines set off in the two dugouts, leaving the main river at length and cutting through smaller tributaries until they were deep into the hot humid swamplands. Nobody liked the idea of cruising around the swamps. It was a bad place to get caught in, a very real danger that if they were ambushed there was little chance of getting out in one piece. The heat and stench of the slimey mud was repulsive. Progress was slow and laborious as they carefully wound their way around the large gnarled roots that protruded from the banks under their craft. Using poles they had cut to push their way along the small tributary - the water was too shallow for the outboards to be used - both boats eased deeper and deeper into the undergrowth. Suddenly, in the leading boat Laker let out a yell and followed it with a full burst from his automatic. From the second craft, Baron, Lee and Lewis thought they were under attack and leapt into the water, scrambling for the shore and flinging themselves down into the muddy morass searching for cover. Seconds later, Laker shouted that there was nothing to worry about now as he'd killed the huge Tiger snake that had landed on the front of his boat.

"Wouldn't fancy getting yomped by that fucker" added Linden.

Turning round, Mackay, about to show the carcass of the snake to the others boat's occupants shouted "Where the bloody hell are the others? Oh Christ, will you look at this lot lads" as he spotted Baron, Lee and Lewis rising from the ground plastered in the stinking mud.

"One of these days Laker, I'm gonna fuck your arse with a fir tree" called Lee wiping the mud from his face.

"What the fuck would you do if one of these bastards nearly fell on top of you?" the indignant Laker replied. "It could've bloody had me for dinner,. Look at the size of it" he pointed out to Baron, also scraping the oozing mud from his front.

"Alright lads. Expect we'd all have done the same in the circumstances. Let's get the bloody hell out of this place. No point going any further now anyway. This lot gives me the shits at the best of times too."

"A pleasure." replied MacKay.

The next two days, the Company stayed on station at Sundar, relieving themselves from the boredom with impromptu games organised by Robson. Football, cricket, volley ball, touch-ball a kind of rough house rugby which resulted in two Mortars retiring hurt after a clash with Laker and Lee and a crib tournament. The total result was unexpectedly a win for the Mortars, their reward being two days excused duty.

"That's just because Robbo was a bloody Mortar Pig once. If we'd won we'd have got fuck all" moaned Linden.

"I don't give a toss really, do you Scouse?" said Lewis.

"Nah. Reckon I can handle it for the next ten days. What's happening in ten days? Well, my very good 'oppo Marine Lewis and myself shall be returning to civilisation about then, so I don't give a fuck, Royal Marines."

"Yeah" chipped in Lewis

"We'll soon be in the Spotlight as pissed as arseoles thinking of our poor dear friends left here, up to their little throats in muck and bullets. Shame ain't it?" he laughed.

"Piss off you two" chided Laker

"Where's Baron?"

"Another O Group with Robbo. Wonder what the fuck they've dreamed up now?"

"Soon find out, here he is now" said Mackay as Baron squeezed into the hut.

"Gather round my ansomes. Come and hear the latest news from the Western Front" he grinned. Settling his large frame down as comfortably as possible on the floor he continued " Well, the buzz is that there's supposed to be about a hundred of these rebel sods around here somewhere, led by the number two in their army, some wally called Yassen Affendi. And we're going to find the sods. The whole Company is going to do a sweep of the area on land and on the rivers and try to drive these buggers into a trap. Won't be easy in this terrain, especially as these sods know every nook and cranny around these parts.

"So what part do we play in this Sarge?" asked Linden.

"Well, we've got to land at a certain point along the river and march inland for a couple of miles, then sweep back in a wide arc towards the river further along and hopefully drive these buggers back into or onto the river where the rest of the unit will be waiting for them."

"Sounds easy enough."

"Except that the two miles we have to march through are all bloody swamp, you'll be delighted to know."

"Balls."

"My sentiments exactly."

"When does all this take place Sarge?"

"First light tomorrow. However, two of you will be delighted to know you're not coming with us. Lee and Lewis. you two sods will stay and keep an eye on things here. You were designated purely because you two are next for repat and someone had to stay behind, so it might as well be you. Something else you have your leader to thank for ." grinned Baron.

"We are forever in your debt" mimicked Lee bowing as gracefully as possible.

"About bloody time we had some perks" smiled Lewis. "Don't worry lads, we'll keep the home fires burning until our brave men return from the Front, eh Scouse?

"When you two have finished taking the piss, I'll carry on" said Baron.

"Now, all we'll take are patrol gear and a few extra hand grenades just in case. So check your weapons tonight, get some scran on the go, then, with a verse or two, we'll all get our heads down."

"Is there anything left in that bloody book we haven't heard yet?" asked Laker.

"One or two, but we can always start again at the beginning if you like" smiled Baron.

"Wonderful."

"Here, I've just thought of a joke" said Moran who had been very quiet in the corner.

"Oh Christ, another gem on the way. Let's have it then, if we have to."

"What's red and hangs from trees?" asked Moran with an impish grin.

"Go on surprise us."

"A monkey's afterbirth." laughed Moran.

"Fucking charming. What kind of brain have you got?"

"If he had a fucking brain he'd be dangerous."

"At first light the Company left on their patrol, a dozen dugouts heading up the river to the point where they were to start their march.

"Watch out for the Tiger snakes, Lakes" called Lee as the MMGs moved out.

"Bollicks." Robson had ordered Lee and Lewis to keep in constant touch with both him and headquarters in Brunei on the A40 set. With the huge aerial they had set up they were able , by carefully tuning in, to pick up the calls from the whole unit spread over the area and although they were unable to make contact with each individual section it made interesting listening to hear the familiar voices relaying their positions which Lee and Lewis plotted on their map to gain an overall picture of the operation. Between their regular calls to Robson and Headquarters their time was spent cleaning up the area and preparing the evening meal for the Company when they returned.

"About time we had a wet ain't it?" asked Lewis.

"You get cracking on that and I'll radio HQ again to keep the buggers happy. Don't want them taking it into their tiny minds to come and pay us a surprise visit, do we?"

"Not exactly going to catch us up to anything are they?"

"Well, I thought we'd have another look at all that lovely green stuff again and maybe count it to make sure none's missing."

"OK. Then we can have a game of cards for big stakes eh?"

"You can sod off Maverick. For once in my life I've got some real dough and I'm buggered if I'm going to lose it to you or any other con artist" replied Lewis.

"I didn't mean a real game, just sort of play friendly like with all the money lying around like it is on the films in Monte Carlo."

"You go and dig it up then while I get the char ready. That's if you remember where we buried it" laughed Lewis.

"That's one thing I'm not likely to forget in a hurry. Back in a flash."

In the days that the Company had been in Sundar it was normal for headquarters in Brunei to send a boat out to them with supplies, mail and ammunition, so when the two heard the distant chug of a motor they were not unduly surprised. Quickly returning their treasure to its hiding place in the ground behind the second basher, they ran to the bank of the river taking precautionary cover until the craft came into sight.

This time it was not marines from the unit that were manning the craft but two Navy ratings in the charge of a Petty Officer. They, it transpired were from a frigate lying off the coast and had been seconded to the Headquarters in Brunei for experience training in handling craft around the rivers and swamplands of Borneo.

Nevertheless anyone who bought supplies and more importantly, mail to the outposts were more than welcome and after the basic introductions and confirmation to Headquarters that the sailors had arrived safely, tea and banter about the latest state of things ensued.

According to the latest 'buzzes' the enemy were now totally dis-organised and trying desperately to escape back over the border to Indonesian territory. Isolated pockets of resistance were still causing problems in various areas which gave rise to the general feeling that this particular war was going to be a long drawn out affair.

Royal Navy frigates were actively engaged in patrolling the Borneo coastline while the Royal Air Force constantly carried out reconnaissance sorties, both services greatly contributing to the success that had been scored. 42 Commando's task was to try and capture some of the higher echelons of the enemy who it was known were still at large in the area trying desperately to escape the net which was closing in on them. While confident that it was only a matter of time before the rebels were caught, the Security Forces were hampered by the reluctance of the local population to assist them - as much as they wanted to - for fear of reprisals from the desperate and ruthless Communists.

"This bastard Affendi is putting the fear of Christ up the locals. He's burned down countless villages and murdered every bugger in sight who's refused to help him and his cronies. Everyone's shit scared of the bugger, so we don't get a lot of help from the kampongs. Still, I'm sure you' booties' will soon have him under lock and key." said the Petty Officer.

"Our lads are out now looking for the bastard." replied Lewis.

"Wouldn't like to be in his shoes if they catch him.

"Yeah." smirked one of the ratings "I hear a few stories over the grapevine that you sods think the Geneva Convention is a meeting of Swiss gentlemen and fuck all to do with the correct treatment of prisoners in wartime."

"When you've been through some of the crap we have and seen your oppos gunned down by these bastards, you'll probably feel likewise" retorted Lee.

"Geneva fucking Convection? Don't make me laugh." he growled.

"Not really the right attitude though, is it?" said the younger of the ratings.

"I mean, say it was you that was captured, you'd expect the proper treatment from them wouldn't you?"

"Where did you get him from?" Lewis asked of the PO. And continuing

"You're living in a dream world sailor and the sooner you realise it the better. How long have you been out here? Is this your first trip abroad? Must be."

"It's my first month ever abroad, but what has that got to do with it?"

"Let me enlighten you sunshine." continued Lewis. "You will soon get to learn that the British serviceman is not the paragon of virtue that the world and the great British public think. When we lost a few blokes at Limbang some of the blokes went a bit crackers; the fear and the pressure all built up and some of them took instant revenge on the enemy that was unlucky enough to get caught. And it wasn't a very pretty sight, either. One or two of the lads are very handy with a knife and bayonet. Ever see a woman's tit hacked off? Or a man lose an ear in one swift movement? Or the agony hot steel can produce if it's placed in the right place? Or the wrong place if you're on the receiving end. Ever seen or heard rather, the sound of a prisoner being interrogated by our 'so British Officers? No, you've got a lot to learn yet sailor. Life on a bloody boat is a bit different from this life. Stick around, you'll see what it's all about."

"I reckon that's difficult to believe, too" said the Petty Officer.

"Your NCOs wouldn't allow that to happen."

"You must be fuckin' joking." said Lee, "They're the worst buggers. Here, Lewy, remember a certain Sergeant who shall remain nameless who got caught in an animal snare that he swore the rebels were responsible for? Nearly lost his bloody foot. Dead lucky. As soon as he was fit to go on patrol again he took a look at a basher in the middle of the ulu and decided that the occupants were going to pay for his pain. So he grabbed this bloke, staked him out on the deck, poured pussers jam over his face and eyes and stood there watching as the ants came and ate it and half of his eyes with it. Mind you, I will admit he's a bit of a vicious bastard at the best of times."

"Fucking sounds like it."

"Perhaps we wouldn't like to be caught by you buggers after all."

"Do you think the enemy are any different?"

"Guess not."

"What do you think this punk Affendi is up to then? Especially now the net is closing in and he's getting desperate."

"Slippery bastard by all accounts" said the PO

"These bastards are so bloody good in the ulu that it's bloody near impossible to catch them. If it wasn't for our Iban trackers we'd get nowhere near them. Mind you, that's a bit of a struggle at times too. A few times they've got to the enemy before the rest of the patrol and just lopped the heads off with their machete. Then they take the heads back and hang them outside their basher as a sign of their manhood. They have to bring the woman they want to live with a head as a token of their bravery, too."

"Nice buggers."

"Jesus."

"Yeah. Get a patrol of them and Johnny Gurkha's together and the fireworks really start. Both bloody brilliant in the ulu though."

"Thank God I joined the Navy"

"Wish to Christ I had sometimes. Nice cushy life floating around on the oggin; plenty of runs ashore in different ports; cheap fags and booze; great life really I suppose." said Lee.

"Not that great" said the heavily tattooed PO shaking his head.

"We do get pissed about a lot. Always on NATO exercises and convoy duties. Buggered about in port too, what with Divisions and parades and all that crap."

"Yeah, true" conceded Lewis.

"All got our little parts to play I suppose."

"Hark at the bloody philosopher!" exclaimed Lee. "Swallowed a bloody dictionary or something?"

"Leave that sort of thing to the Deck Apes" replied Lewis grinning at the sailors.

"Anyway, time we were making a move I reckon" said the PO

"Must get back in time for tots,"

"Hark at them" said Lee. "Bloody Pusser's rum and a nice comfortable billet waiting for them and they reckon they've got it rough.

"Can't go without our tot even if we are ashore for a while. Be a bloody mutiny if they stopped that" the dark, thick set older rating replied.

"Go on then, shove off. And take this mail with you for us, OK?

"OK Royal. Catch you up at HQ probably if you're due to repat soon."

"Right. We'll sniff you out round about tot time" said Lee.

"By all means."

"See you Royal." Settling into the dugout, the three sailors with the PO at the rear with the Bren Gun pushed off from the bank, started the motor and chugged off downstream.

"Don't forget that mail" yelled Lee after them.

Watching the boat round the bend, Lee daydreamed for an instant of when he and Lewis would make that same trip; their first step on the way back to Blighty.

Seconds later his daydreams and the silence were shattered by the burst of automatic fire coming from the direction the boat had taken. Immediately Lewis was alongside him.

"What the fuck was that?" he asked.

"Fuck knows." They could still hear the distant chugging of the outboard but now, instead of becoming quieter the noise was increasing.

"I reckon they've been ambushed. Dunno if it's them coming back or some other sod in the boat now."

"Only heard one burst of fire; perhaps they got whoever they saw."

"Could be. Can't take chances though. Get into the ulu over there then if there's bother we've got them in a cross-fire. Hurry." As Lee dashed over to the protecting jungle Lewis lined the sights of his gun firmly on the corner of the river that the boat would show. At last it chugged around the bend and came into sight and Lewis instantly saw that it was still occupied by the sailors. But something was wrong for from his position Lewis could only see two of them.

"Scouse, get over here." he yelled to his companion.

"What's up? Have they been ambushed?"

"Dunno yet. Hang on, what's the PO shouting?" Waving his arms frantically while trying to steer a straight course, the PO was shouting at the top of his voice for help.

"What the fuck does he want?"

"A medic. He's shouting for a medic."

"He knows there's no medic here."

"But they must've run into some bother. Get the first aid kit, quick someone must be hurt. I can't see the other matelot." As the boat edged into the bank Lewis saw the remaining sailor slumped in the bottom of the boat in a pool of blood. "Fuck me, what happened?" The PO burst into an uncontrollable fit of crying and shaking.

"Stop that crap and tell me what happened" shouted Lewis at the same time trying to get to the injured sailor. Then he noticed that the other rating was also covered in blood.

"It was a terrible accident" wailed the PO.

"What are you fucking on about. Help me get these two out, man." Just then Lee arrived. "Fucking hell, what happened?"

"Thank Christ you're back Scouse. Give me a hand here will you this arseole's cracked up and useless" he said nodding towards the PO.

Easing the first sailor out onto the bank, the two turned back to his injured companion while the PO held the boat steady against the bank.

"Lay him here and give him a jab, quick. Come on sailor, give us hand and pull your fucking self together before there's another casualty. What the hell happened?"

"I couldn't help it really. It just went off."

"Oh great. That's all we need. A fucking matelot playing with a Bren Gun. Jesus."

"It was an accident."

"Shut up and get out of the way. Fuck off over there and admire your handiwork."

"Alright Scouse, that'll do. He's in shock too that's for sure."

"He'll get more than bloody shock later." Now they assessed the extent of the sailor's injuries. The one up forward had been hit in the back, just above the hip and was in a very serious condition. And he was unconscious. The other had received a terrible wound in the ankle which was hardly hanging together. Still groaning with shock and pain, the morphine was quickly taking effect but Lewis and Lee recognised that there was not a lot more they could do for the men.

"Get on the blower quick Scouse. Tell HQ what's happened and ask what else we can do to help these poor bastards."

"Right."

"And bring a couple of blankets back with you." Lewis called after his companion. Covering the gaping wound on the sailor's ankle with his shirt, Lewis ordered the PO to remove his shirt also and wrap it against the blood seeping from the back of the unconscious man. Gently talking to the other, Lewis assured him that help was on the way.

"Want to tell me what happened now?" Lewis turned to the trembling PO.

"Get it off your chest for fucks sake."

"We'd just got round the bend and as it's not so far up to Brunei I thought I'd have a quick go with the gun, y'know, just to say I'd actually fired the thing on active service."

"Fuck me" groaned Lewis.

"Well, I slowed down and pointed the gun over the stern and fired a couple of shots into the water."

"Jesus."

"Then, then....."

"Go on, get on with it."

"Well , I thought I'd put the safety catch on but as I lowered the gun into the bottom of the boat another burst just.....well.... sort of....went off. It was awful. An accident. I didn't mean to shoot them. They'll be alright, won't they? I could see the lads were hit and I panicked and didn't know what to do so I turned the boat round and came back here....what am I going to do?..... I didn't do it on purpose......what will happen to me now...... They will be OK won't they?" Sobbing again and in deep shock, Lewis knew there was no point chastising the distraught PO so he tried to console him.

"No good getting too uptight now. They'll be OK I'm sure. Just keep your cool until help arrives. Won't be long now."

"They'll send me to prison, won't they?" stammered the sailor.

"No they won't but you'd better steel yourself for an official investigation and a court-martial."

"But it was an accident. I swear it."

"Accident my arse" said Lee as he returned. Gross negligence you bastard. For two pins I'd put a bullet through your stupid head and save them the bother. Should never give fucking matelots guns in the first place."

"OK Scouse, that's enough. What did HQ say?"

"Two choppers on the way right now with a medic. Should be here any minute. One of us will have to go with one of them because most of HQ are involved in this chase for Affendi and there's no bugger left there."

"Alright, I'll go with them. When we fuck off keep close to that radio. They're bound to bring me straight back as you'll be alone. So I won't be long."

"Right. How are these two poor bastards now?"

"Well, this one is still unconscious, but I think I've stopped the bleeding. He's had a shot so there's nothing else we can do until the medic gets here. The other one's in a bad state of shock but the morphine's taken effect so he's as comfortable as we can make him right now. Wish the bloody choppers would hurry up." Minutes later they heard the drone of the helicopter engines racing towards them and almost instantly they were hovering over the field where Lee was bringing them in. Racing from the first to land, the medic, clutching his bag reached the men and Lewis who gave him a report on what had happened. Assessing the injuries instantly, the Leading Sick Berth Attendant signalled the chopper pilots that they were not to cut their engines. Lee had unloaded two stretchers from the aircraft and brought them to the men.

"They've both had a shot of morphine and the flow of blood seems to have stopped" said Lewis.

"Good. They're in a bad way though. let's get them on the stretchers right away. Strap them on and load up the choppers. Who's coming with us?"

"Me." replied Lewis.

"OK, let's get going. No time to waste by the look of it."

"PO, you'd better come with me" added the LSBA.

Placing the two injured men on the stretchers and covering them with blankets Lee and Lewis grabbed one stretcher and the LSBA and the PO the other and ran to the door of the choppers, loading each one onto the floor of the aircraft.

"See you later" yelled Lee above the roar of the aircraft.

"Look after that bloody cash my son. Won't do a bunk with it, will you?" responded Lewis.

"Where the fuck to?" laughed Lee. "Seeyuh." Lewis strapped himself into the stick leader's seat and put on the headphones to make radio contact with the pilot, but as was often the case the radio was out of order so Lewis smartly tapped the pilot on the ankle which was just above Lewis's head to indicate that all was OK for takeoff.

Quickly the two choppers lifted off on Lee's guidance, turned due East and headed for Brunei. Lewis tried several times to make radio contact with the pilot but the radio was definitely unworkable and he reluctantly gave up, keeping the headphones on just in case. Resignedly he looked out the open doorway at the rivers and jungle below and at the injured sailor at his feet. Lewis reckoned that the chances of the sailor surviving were limited. The SBA had not spent too much time on him, though Lewis estimated that there was not a lot he could do there in the middle of nowhere; an operating theatre was necessary as soon as possible to remove the bullets from his back. Unless it was already too late. For all Lewis could tell now, the sailor may be dead. The wind rushing in from the door of the chopper and the noise of the engines made it impossible for Lewis to judge whether the sailor was breathing or not. The effects of the morphine would still render him unconscious and out of pain at least, reasoned Lewis.

Gazing down at the swirling river they were passing over Lewis's thoughts strayed to the remainder of the Company and he wondered how they were getting on in the chase for Yassin Affendi. He didn't in the least envy them their task as the ground they were covering was almost totally swampland which they all hated. The sucking, clinging mud, totally swampland which they all hated. The mud, mosquitoes, snakes and the stench of the filthy water mixed with their sweat plus the awful prospect that at any moment they could come under fire from an unseen enemy made even the thought of such an environment extremely distasteful and highly dangerous. Thank God thought Lewis that they now had barely eight days left before leaving for Brunei and the first stage home.

Lewis was snatched from his day dream dramatically and alarmingly as suddenly the sailor on the stretcher whom he had believed to be totally unconscious raised his head as far as he could above the straps that were holding his stretcher down and mouthed something to Lewis. Unable to hear or comprehend what the man was saying and completely taken off his guard that the sailor should be conscious let alone able to sit up, Lewis' immediate reaction was to grab the intercom and try and make contact with the pilot. But the radio was still out of action and Lewis could now decipher what it was the man wanted. He was evidently cold as a result of the wind rushing into the chopper through the open doorway and lifting the blankets covering him, and wanted Lewis to cover him up properly.

Motioning with his hands and mouth that he understood what the man was saying Lewis wondered what the hell he was going to do next. He had no contact with the pilot and was therefore unable to tell him to keep a steady course, for if he was to help the sailor and make him more comfortable he would have to unstrap himself and move across to the stretcher to tuck the blankets in. But, should the pilot suddenly change course it was quite likely that Lewis would be thrown right out the open doorway.

There was nothing to do but take a chance he decided. They had been in the air barely ten minutes so it must be another five until they reached Brunei and started their descent when the chopper was most likely to swerve and alter course as it settled towards the ground.

There was also one or two racks around the sides of the chopper plus the actual framework and structure of the craft that he could cling to as he crossed to the sailor. And the least he could do was try and make the poor sod as comfortable as possible, he reasoned.

Making good his resolve, Lewis unstrapped himself from the seat, took off his headphones and grabbing the sides of the chopper, tentatively made his way the short distance to the stretcher. Reaching it, he realised that this was the most tricky part for he now had to let go of the rack he was holding on to, bend down and with both hands try to tuck the blanket under the man. Silently praying that the pilot would hold a steady course for the next few seconds, Lewis quickly pushed the blankets as far under the sailor as he could, sweating profusely even though the wind rushing in through the open doorway beat against his face. Having done the best job he could, Lewis stood up and grabbed hold of the rack again with one hand while the other groped for another hand hold. Not an instant too soon he managed to find one, for his calculations had been slightly out and the pilot had, in the emergency, increased his speed to such an extent that they were now banking hard to starboard and with a lurch commencing their descent. The gaping hole of the doorway was now almost parallel to the ground as Lewis clung on with all his strength to save himself being thrown out. Finally levelling out the chopper eased its way to the ground as Lewis flung himself into his seat and sat gasping for breath as the perspiration coursed down his face and body.

Immediately a team of medics was at the doorway of the helicopter and with Lewis' help the stretcher was unstrapped and rushed to the waiting ambulances. Shaken by his experience, Lewis sat back for a few seconds as the chopper cut its engines. Over at the edge of the sports field that was acting as the chopper pad Lewis could see some marines from Headquarters Company that he knew and he alighted from the aircraft and headed for them.

"Back here again Lewy?" called one of the familiar faces.

"Off on repat this time?"

"No such luck Willie. Just brought those two matelots in from Sundar. Poor bastards, don't give much hope for the one I came back with. Frightened the bloody life out of me in the chopper though."

"How's that?" Lewis related the incident to his companion as they walked across to the school building which acted as Headquarters.

"Took a bloody chance didn't you? And so near repat."

"What the hell could I do?"

"Yeah. Rather you than me though. Want a quick brew before you go back?"

"Good idea. I could use something after that little lot. Can't hang about though. Ol' Scouse is out there on his own so they'll be off any minute I reckon." Lewis perched himself on the end of Willie Patterson's bed as the cleric fetched a steaming mug of tea from the far end of the room where a small stove was located. "Here, throw this down you."

"Cheers" said Lewis taking a good swig of the brew. "Christ, what the hell have you got in this?" he asked as the burning liquid coursed down his parched throat.

"Don't tell me you've forgotten the delicate bouquet of Pusser's Rum already?" quizzed Patterson.

"Never happen, my son, but its been a while since it arrived in these quantities. We've been drinking that local shit since Limbang. Not bad really but not exactly Pussers. Better than fuck all I guess. Needless to say Marine Lee is well hooked on the stuff" he grinned.

"Surprise, surprise" laughed Patterson. "Is he still chasing all the local virgins?"

"Naturally. That bastard'll never change. Same as me though, can't wait to get back to Singers and UK .How're the repats going? On time?"

"Usually a few days late, but not too bad. I keep a good lookout for your two names. By the way, you owe me."

"What for?"

"Didn't you find it a strange coincidence that you two were booked on the same flight to UK?" laughed Patterson.

"You crafty bastard. Cheers. I'll remember you in my will."

"Fat chance."

"Bloody quiet around here today; no interrogations to keep the Gestapo happy?"

"No, everyone's out on this hunt for Affendi and his oppos. From what I hear over at the signals post they're not having much luck, either. The crafty bastard's giving us a bloody headache and no mistake."

"We'll get him eventually, no sweat."

"He'll be halfway to the border by now I reckon."

"Dunno. That's where everyone expects him to go, but I reckon he's trying to lay low for a while and sneak across later."

"Could be. What's up Jimmy?" said Lewis to the gawky young marine who entered the room.

"Choppers ready to take you back to Sundar Lewy."

"Shit. Don't hang about, do they? Still old Scouse is back there on his tod so I'd better get back and look after him."

"Give him my regards and tell him to leave some of the virgins for the rest of us."

"No chance of that."

"Take this with you then" said Patterson throwing Lewis two huge bars of chocolate.

"Cheers. Where'd you get these then? You're worse than bloody Baron."

"How is the bugger? Still organising?"

"Yeah, naturally. He's bloody good though; we'd be a bit lost without the sod. But don't tell him I said so."

"Has he lost any weight?"

"We've all lost bloody weight."

"Yeah; still never mind. Soon be on that big silver bird, eh?"

"Can't come quick enough."

"See you later then. Take it easy."

"Cheers Willie. Could be back in a week or so. Have a good piss up before we go, OK?"

"You're on. See yuh." Crossing to the aircraft Lewis informed the Naval aircrew rating waiting to guide the chopper up that the radio was not working but was told that this was already known and they were waiting for parts to be flown out direct from Singapore. A minute later he was in the air and on the way back to Sundar.

"Still in one piece then Scouse?" said Lewis on his arrival back at the camp.

"Fought them all off single handed did you" he laughed.

"Something like that. Just come across the radio that the matelot that got hit in the back just died. Poor bastard."

"Christ. That PO will be in the shit now alright."

"So he bloody should be. Probably get slung out before some bastard tops him."

"How's the other one?"

"They reckon he'll lose his foot."

"Jesus. All because some dozy bastard wanted to fire a gun on active service. Makes you wanna puke, eh?"

"Must've been fate I reckon"

"Fate be fucked. Discipline, or the lack of it. Fucking matelots."

"Oh well, no good getting uptight about it. We did all we could for them."

"Yeah. Though I can't help thinking how much worse it is for them and their families than it was for our lads that got shot up. At least they were killed in action and not pissing about on a river with no bastard within miles."

"That's what I mean, fate"

"Where does fate start then? At birth? Are we fated then to do every single thing that we do? Is that right?"

"Dunno. Maybe we're all meant to live a certain life and meet certain people who will determine our destiny on this planet and influence every decision we make?"

"On the other hand" said Lewis "We could be totally responsible for planning our own lives and all the fuck ups we make are no-one's fault but our own."

"I went to a bloody Spiritualist meeting one night in Pompey, quite by accident as it happens 'cos I thought it was a lecture on other planets. Anyway, this geezer started ranting and raving and everybody started singing bloody Harry Krishna. The lights went out and we were sat in a semi circle, about fifteen of us, listening to this bloke wailing away. This went on for nearly a bloody hour and they were all getting worked up something rotten. I wanted to piss off because there was a Cup match on the tele but I didn't want to disturb no bugger so I stuck it out. Anyway, to cut a story short the singing all stopped and lights

180

went on again and there was this Madonna with a crucifix in the centre of the floor. I never saw any bastard put it there and it certainly wasn't there when we started. Bloody spooky. Maybe I nodded off, but I don't think so. Then the bloke who was conducting this lot started to ask everyone in turn what they'd seen while all the singing was going on. Some of the answers were bloody amazing. One bloke thought the Madonna had sat on his lap and told him his life story; another said he watched the Madonna pass from person to person, me included, kissing their foreheads; some old dear reckoned she felt thirty years younger and that all her aches and pains had disappeared instantly. And so on. Then the bloke started telling everyone that the spirits would do great things for them and asked everybody what they thought about it all. Well, when he got to me I said I thought it was all mass hysteria and I hadn't seen anything at all. He told me then that I was a very determined person capable of reaching high planes. I was just about due a draft at the time so I thought he must be referring to a bloody RAF Britannia. But he meant the astral planes I guess because then he said that I was constantly watched over by a woodchopper, yeah a bloody woodchopper. I said the only bloody woodchopper I'd met was on Dartmoor and in this day and age didn't anticipate meeting any more. But he said this woodchopper was my spiritual guide and he would lead me through life and help me make the right decisions for the rest of my earthly days. Right bloody creepy it was. Apparently all of us have a guide like that, so he said."

"Well I don't think much of that guide the poor bloody matelot had and our blokes as well."

"Yeah, but it may all be part of some master plan."

"What the fuck are you on about?"

"Well, maybe the guides we are all supposed to have are put there by God to watch us and sort of report to Him what we get up to and then when we snuff it, he decides whether we get to Heaven or go Down Under."

"Not that religious crap again, please."

"Well, it's possible ain't it?"

"Look, there's a standard argument I always give about religion. I even confused the fuckin' Padre one night on the rare occasion that

181

he collared me in the barrack room. It was a rare occasion that he was bloody sober, too. I always say that God, so the bible says, put Adam and Eve on Earth in the beginning, right?"

"Yeah, so?"

"Well, it then says that Adam and Eve had a little bit of nookie and knocked out two sprogs, Cain and Abel, OK?"

"Right."

"Next it says the Cain and Abel went off and found themselves a couple of wives and got hitched. Now, if Adam and Eve were the first people on earth, where the fuck did Cain and Abel find two bits of stuff to get hitched to?"

"Dunno really." And then I said to the Padre 'who made God then'?

"What did he say to that?"

"He coughed and spluttered and said he had a bloody bible class to attend to. Told me to come and see him later. Knew I wouldn't bother. Used to give me bloody funny looks when I saw him though."

"They reckon he was screwing the CO's daughter too."

"Why not? Every other fucker in the Pigs Mess was, so why should he dip out?"

"Dirty old bastard."

"Lucky old bastard."

"Suppose we'd better get some grub on the go; the lads'll be back before it gets dark I reckon."

"Yeah , they won't piss about in the ulu and the mangroves in the dark."

"No news about Affendi yet then?"

"Last I heard on the radio was that Headquarters think he's split his gang up and he's just got ten or so hard core left with him. All armed to the teeth apparently."

"Shouldn't fancy bumping that lot in the dark."

"Pass that can spanner. Fancy a bit of Irish stew tonight by way of a change?"

"Roll on fucking repat."

"Talking of which, is our treasure trove OK?"

"Yeah , I checked it while you were away. No sweat."

"Had a nice day out then Sarge?"

"That was one little exercise you don't know how lucky you were to miss. Reckon we must've covered at least twenty miles through the bloody ulu and swamps today lads, eh?" Baron asked of his weary men.

"That and a bit more I'd say" said Laker. "I'm bleedin' knackered. Those swamps are bastard places. And all for fuck all too."

"Not really; at least we know the buggers' split up his gang so if we do come across him he'll have less to fight us with."

"Don't think we'll ever get him without burning the whole bloody ulu down." said Linden.

"Ah well, tomorrow's another day. Let's have a few hands and a couple of verses to boost your flagging morale and send you all to sleep." grinned Baron.

"I won't need sod all to get me to kip." replied Moran.

"Look at the size of this bastard" exclaimed Mackay enticing the head of a large bull leech from his leg with a cigarette end. "The sod's got more blood than I have."

"Yeah, and he looks pretty pissed on it too." laughed Baron.

"I shan't miss those buggers when we piss off." said Lee.

"Yeah" agreed Lewis. "Remember when we were here on exercise Scouse? Every morning we had to do a five mile run at six in the bloody morning and it always ended at a bridge about half a mile up the river from where we were camped and we had to dive in and swim back to the base. By the time we'd done this for two mornings all the fuckin' leeches in Borneo used to line up in the water waiting for us. You could actually see the bastards licking their bloody lips."

"Didn't know leeches had lips" said an incredulous Laker. "Throw one of them over Jock."

"Laker, Birmingham College of Knowledge reading Biology" stated Lee to the amusement of all.

"What a fucking doughnut."

"That was a bloody good exercise really" continued Lewis.

"We had a great volleyball league going and naturally the Scots won it and the two crates that went with it."

"That's right" added Lee. and they 'paid out' the day we had our one and only run shore in a place called Kota Belud. What a bloody

183

run that was too. Shit. Me and Lewy were in the unit team and they fixed up a game with the local heroes, but by the time we'd had our share of the winnings and a gutful at the one and only bar in the town we were bloody paralytic.

"Yeah, ever see three hundred bootnecks in one bar? Fuckin' chaos."

"That's right. The bloody Provo Marshall, a big bastard at that time called Burley, and was he ever, had to march the whole mob of us down to the football pitch and he stuck us all at one end as far away as he could from the opposition, though that didn't last long."

"And us two were in the middle of this lot happily knocking back the cans until someone reminded us that we were playing." laughed Lee.

"Who won then?" asked Moran.

"The Royal Corps, of course. Even though we only had nine men."

"Why only nine?"

"Us two got sent off. He thumped the goalie as usual and I scored one of the all time great goals but the bloody stupid referee we had insisted it was offside. So I hit him a cracker on the nut with the ball. Fucking locals went bananas. Nearly had a riot on our hands. The CO and all the pigs were there with the local mafia and they weren't exactly thrilled either."

"Mind you, he got a bloody shock on the way back to base that night as well, eh?"

"What happened there then?"

"Well, after the game everyone went back to the bar and continued pissing up. Things got out of hand after a punch up so the 2 I/C ordered everybody back to camp. All the three tonners were lined up and the bodies hurled in. The convoy must've stopped a dozen or more times to let blokes out for a spew or a piss or both at the same time in some cases."

"It was just like 'After Blenheim' Sarge; Rudyard would have loved it" laughed Lewis.

"I'm sure he would" grinned Baron.

"Anyway, we'd just loaded up after a stoppage and moved off when this land-rover flashes us down. So we stopped and then this bloody head poked itself over the tall-board and started bollicking us for throwing things out the back. And some bugger, no one ever found out who, planted a beautiful right hook smack on this sod's nose and sends him sprawling in the mud. Everyone shouted and banged the drivers cabin so he pissed off, naturally. Well, for a mile or so anyway before the bloody land-rover caught us up. We all got turfed out but everyone was so pissed, there was no chance of anyone getting any sense from us so we were told to fuck off."

"The thing was that it was the bloody Adjutant that had stuck his head over the tailboard and got a big right." laughed Lee.

"Yeah, but he had his bloody revenge though. Support Company was Duty Company for the duration of the exercise."

"And the bastard made us do a man pack march halfway up Mount Kinabalu, the highest mountain in bloody Borneo.

"We were fucking glad to get away from Borneo in the end and even that was a bloody strain. We got stuck at Jesselton airport for 36 hours waiting for the bleedin' RAF to get a Beverley out to us; sat in a so-called lounge with no air conditioning, or fan, or fuck all. Like a day in a bloody oven. Bridge over the river Kwai was fuck all on that place.

"Yeah. Still, another wonderful experience to write home about. One day I'll write a bloody book about this lot."

"You've got a job to write your bloody name, never mind sod all else."

"Balls."

"Is that your family motto?"

"Very droll. What's on the menu for tomorrow then sarge?

"Dunno yet" replied Baron. "Should be an admin day after that last effort, but I doubt it knowing bloody Robbo.

"He's been on the radio for ages" said Laker re-entering the room.

"Probably getting the latest on Affendi."

"Could be. Anyway, heads down time I reckon lads. Now, would you prefer some Soldier and Sailor Too, or something a bit more saucy?"

"What like No Nose's crutch piece when she's on blob?"

"You're a crude bastard at times Lakes" said Lee.

"Gordon Bennet, hark who's talking."

"So much for the admin day lads. Guess which platoon has been volunteered for a little sortie into the middle of the bloody swamps again?" Baron said as he returned from O Group.

"Shit, no."

"Fraid so Scouser. You and Lewy an' all. It'll be your last effort though because we're going out for three days. Bloody hell, that's all we need at this stage of training" moaned Lewis. "Tell us the worst then Sarge."

"Well, apparently they haven't had any luck trying to catch our friend Affendi, so the new tactic is to let him come to us. That means all the platoons are going to be dropped at various locations where the powers that be think it possible that Affendi holes up now and again. Just a case of sitting there and waiting for him to turn up. Then try and capture him alive, But nor necessarily if you get my drift. If he gets in my sights I'll blast him from here to bloody Boogey Street. The object is to try and get some information out of him if we can, so don't anybody get too trigger happy, understand?"

"Correct, Jock, but he's got fuck all to lose now so he's more dangerous than ever in a sense."

"When do we fuck off then Sarge?" asked a concerned Lewis.

"First light. So all get your gear on the ball right now."

"What are we taking then sarge?"

"Minimum. The big radio, arms and ammo, a few grenades, and what you stand in. No packs or fuck all, OK?" Lewis glanced uneasily at Lee, then said "Can't we take a couple of things in a pack just to make life a bit more comfortable?"

"No. Three days without a bed won't hurt you will it? Bloody commandos aren't we? Or supposed to be." added Baron.

"Yeah."

Lee signalled Lewis to step outside the billet while they were all preparing their weapons for the following day. "So what the hell are we going to do with the stuff then?" he whispered.

"Fucked if I know. Can't leave it lying around here for some bugger to nick, that's for sure."

"We'll have to bury it then, somehow."

"How can we explain walking out the hut with our packs right in front of every bastard?"

"Dunno. The only thing is to get out at night when they're all asleep."

"And get out heads blown off by the sentries?"

"That's a point. Hang on, let me think."

"Here, I know. Breakfast is the answer. When they all go over to the galley for scran, we'll grab the stuff and a shovel and make out we're going for a crap in the bushes, then bury the stuff."

"Don't think it's a good idea for both of us to go at the same time, do you? I know, I'll say you've got the shits. Too bad if they don't believe it, but no bugger's going to come and look for you, are they?"

"Sounds OK, but what do I do for Nosh then?" asked Lee,

"Nosh, at a time like this? Fuck the food, the stuff is more important. Ok, I'll get you a sarnie or something."

"Better than fuck all I suppose" groaned Lee.

"Think of all the bloody steaks you'll be able to afford in the Spotlight when we get back."

"S'pose so. I'd better draw a little map after I've buried it just in case I forget where I put it, and we'll stow that in our packs until we get back."

"Good idea, son."

"All OK?"

"Yeah, no problem. Anybody say anything?"

"No, not really. Baron had a good laugh as usual. Did you make sure it was well covered with the plastic?"

"Of course. It's as safe as houses. Let me quickly draw a map and explain it to you."

Half an hour later a small flotilla of six dugouts headed up river from Sundar to the mangrove swamps. Two sections were dropped off at strategic positions at the intersections of rivers before it was the turn of the machine gunners.

"Right lads, this is it" said Baron. Waving a cheery goodbye to the remaining three craft as they sped away, the marines scanned the shoreline at either side of them."

"This is what?" asked Moran. "Where the hell are we supposed to hole up? There's nothing but a straight river bank, no tributaries or fuck all."

"Look again, my son" said Baron. "Under those trees" he said pointing to a large cluster overhanging the main river. "There's a small tributary there, or bloody should be if the map Robbo gave me is on the ball."

"I wouldn't count on that either" remarked Laker.

"Didn't know you could count at all, Lakes" laughed Luther in an unexpected burst of humour.

"Who pulled your fuckin' chain?"

"OK you two. We're not going to find out fuck all sitting here like prize pricks. Head for the bank Jock and we'll have a shuftie." ordered Baron. "That tributary should lead into the swamps for about a half mile and then there should be a woodcutter's hut right at the end of the stream." he continued as MacKay guided the boat towards the bank.

"Is that where we have to hole out and wait Sarge?" asked Lee.

"Yeah."

"I reckon we'll have to paddle through most of that or we'll run out of cotter pins if we use the engine" said Mackay.

"Probably, but we'll give it a go first" replied Baron.

Slowly penetrating the lush undergrowth, the craft was quickly swallowed up in the jungle and completely invisible from the river, Already they were aware of the abundance of Tiger snakes coiled on the foliage above them as they slowly edged deeper and deeper into the undergrowth.

"This place gives me the shits" said Lee.

"Thought you already had them" replied Baron.

In another ten yards they had broken two pins at the base of the propeller shaft, so the idea of using the engine from there on was abandoned.

"Have we got anymore nails?" asked Mackay.

"Waste of time, Jock. Forget it."

"I reckon there's about fifty million bloody leeches on the end of my chopper" whispered Laker. "I can feel the bastards."

"They must be bleeding small buggers then" added Lee.

"Ha bloody ha."

"How much further?" asked Lewis.

"Can't be much further" responded Baron. "Everyone out the boat we'll have to leg it . You can tow the boat Scouser, alright?"

"And if I say no?"

"Tough. Keep yer powder dry my ansomes." said Baron lifting his rifle above his head as he sank into the thick, oozing mud and water,

"Fuckin' mossies" moaned Laker.

"Keep going lads" muttered Baron. "Nearly there I reckon."

"Where've I heard that before?" The light ahead started to improve as the platoon edged forward and the filters of light penetrating the darkness of the overhead foliage assisted their progress.

"That could be what we're looking for up ahead" Baron whispered as he nodded towards a well constructed log cabin on the bank ahead and to their left. "Keep your eyes peeled, There could be some bugger waiting for us. We'll wait here a minute and watch the place for a while." Signalling the remainder to melt into the surrounding foliage, they scanned the area for the slightest signs of activity, but none was forthcoming. The sweat and steam rising from their bodies was soon lost in the humid air and thick undergrowth. Then on Baron's signal they started to edge towards the hut. Suddenly, a flurry to their right had them pressing against the banks looking for cover, but it was only a bird startled by their stealthy approach.

"No need to worry now, Sarge. That sod wouldn't be here if there was anyone else around."

"Yeah, more than likely you're right Jock, but don't let's take any chances, eh? Split up and approach the cabin from both ends. And look out for booby traps" Baron ordered.

The cabin was set in a fifty yard semi circular clearing on the bank; it was a strong construction with a doorway on the riverside and two windows at each end. Quickly, the two groups converged on the building and confirmed its emptiness. Deftly searching all along its length for traps the marines soon satisfied themselves and Baron that all was OK. Posting Moran and Linden at each end as lookouts, Baron and the others made themselves as comfortable as they could inside.

"First thing, get the radio on the ball and contact HQ. Rig the aerial at the top of the hut" ordered Baron firmly settling himself into one corner,

"What time are we supposed to check in?"

"As soon as we're in position."

"I suppose there could be worse ways to spend the last few days of your commission" said Lewis. "At least we've got a bloody roof over our heads this time."

"Light up a fag someone. Must be all the fucking leeches in Borneo on me" moaned Laker. "Look at the bastards, everywhere."

"Is that bloody tea ready yet Scouser?" asked Baron.

"Why am I always duty char waller?"

"cos you've got that certain something that it takes, my son."

"Bullshit."

"That's what rules the Corps, my son."

"Thought it was organisation?"

"That too, of course."

"I should be OK for a job with the bloody NAAFI after this bloody commission. I'd like to know just how many brews I've made in the last eighteen months" pondered Lee.

"How's that radio coming on then Jock?"

"No joy yet. Can't get a bloody bean on it yet."

"Keep going my son. Just a question of time and your technical skill" chided Baron.

"I reckon there must be something wrong somewhere. I've tried all the different calibrations, but no joy so far."

"Well the set was OK when we tested it last night. Didn't get any water in it did we?"

"Nah. Could be the bloody aerial I suppose. Better get up on the roof and have a look I guess."

"Are we out of range?" asked Moran.

"These coaxalls are supposed to give us over fifty miles in this country. We can't be half of that from HQ".

"Nah, must be something else. Let me check it anyway."

"Bloody charming. So what happens if we run into Affendi and need some help?" asked laker.

"Good question, Worry about that when the time comes."

"What happened to good old organisation?"

"Never fear, my sons, Sarge will look after you all" grinned Baron.

"Any joy yet Jock?"

"Not a whisper. Dead as a doornail. Can't think of anything else to try, either."

"Oh well. Look on the bright side; at least we won't have bloody Robbo on our backs for a few days" said Lewis.

"Fuck Robbo" said Linden. "What about if we get attacked?"

"Better get outside lads and get some fire positions sorted out just in case" ordered Baron. "Come on, won't take a minute." Organising the platoon with an individual axis of fire, Baron eventually satisfied himself that the platoon was well able to defend itself should they be attacked and to this end he rehearsed them for half an hour in getting to the positions on the double."

"Now it's time for some bronzey bronzey" said Lewis peeling off his sweat stained shirt. "Care to join me Marine Lee?"

"Well, as we'll be winging our way to the UK shortly" he said in a voice loud enough for all to hear

"I just might."

"No you won't you're on watch" laughed Baron.

"Both of you. Move."

For the next two days the platoon amused themselves in the main with countless hands of Bridge, at Baron's insistence, sunbathing, and in the case of Moran cutting up dead Tiger snakes and using the skins to scare the life out of Linden and Laker who were the two who disliked the reptiles most.

Finally, their last day dawned.

"Thank Christ we're pissing off tonight" said Laker.

"I could eat a pusser's ship's cat I'm so bloody hungry."

"Lakes, the day you're not hungry war will break out. I've never known any sod eat like you. Bloody gannet" said Baron.

"I'm a growing lad."

"From the neck up."

"Funny."

"And don't forget you owe me twenty bucks before you piss off to

Singers."

"What for?"

"How conveniently he forgets. The night we left Singers you had a twenty off me in the NAAFI for going to Nee Soon, before we got the buzz about this little trip, remember?"

"Oh yeah. Thought you'd forgotten about that."

"No chance."

"Talking of owing money, reminds me of a little story." said Baron.

"Here we go again....."

"No, really. Bloody funny as it happens. There was this old Assault Engineer in Palestine when we was there; Old Harry Glynn. Right old sod he was. Been through all the wars, Korea, Suez and probably the bloody Boer War if the truth be known. Anyway, there was this German bloke attached to us and for some reason old Harry lent him some money one night when they was both pissed. Had to be pissed, he didn't like the bloody Gerries after the war and all that. But this bloody Hun wouldn't give Harry his cash back for ages and he was a great big bastard, so Harry wasn't about to get stuck into him in a hurry. So what the crafty old sod did was one night, when the Hun was flaked out in his pit, pissed, Harry wired up his bed with dynamite and PE and had the wires leading out to a plunger in the centre of the room.

He squatted there with his two hands on the top of the plunger and got one of the lads to shake the Hun. As soon as the bastard had his eyes open old Harry asked him for his cash. Course, the bloody Gerry wasn't too happy anyway at getting woken up, but he bloody soon sobered up when Harry said 'check under your bed fuckin' Nazi. Unless you pay me back my money right now I'm gonna blow your fuckin' bed back to Berlin with you in it' Christ, you've never seen anyone shit themselves that quickly in your life. He reached into his locker and threw Harry a wad of notes. Then Harry said out loud 'death to the Third Reich' and shoved down on the plunger. Well, the bloody Hun actually left his pit and fucking near hit the ceiling. Of course the dynamite wasn't connected, but he wasn't to know was he? Laugh, we nearly wet our bloody selves."

"Didn't the Hun clobber Harry then?" asked Lewis.

"Nah. He knew bloody well that Harry could do that at any time he felt like it, so he kept stum. Never borrowed fuck all off anyone again though." At that moment, MacKay, who had been on watch slipped into the cabin.

"Sarge, I think we've got company on the way. Damn sure I can hear a motor stopping and starting up river."

"OK lads, action stations. Take your lead from me if it comes to firing. Just might be one of ours."

"Let's go"

Quickly taking up their positions crouched in the undergrowth and behind cover, the marines waited and listened; now the noise of an engine could clearly be heard approaching their position.

"It's cut out again" whispered Mackay to Baron.

"Probably having the same trouble we did."

"Think it's one of our lot?"

"Fucked if I know. Could be."

"How far do you reckon they are away now?"

"Not that far. Have to start legging it soon."

"If its Affendi, we could be in for a good scrap."

"That's only a small engine, so it can't be a very big boat, so there won't be many in it, that's for sure."

"Hang on, it's stopped again. Sounded close as well."

No sooner had MacKay spoken than the sound of the outboard motor spluttering into life reached them. Only this time the sound was racing away from them.

"The bastards are pissing off" said Baron.

"Yeah, and do you know why?"

"Why?"

"Because they've seen that bloody great aerial sticking up from the top of the hut, that's why."

"So it must've been some bugger who didn't want to make contact with the military" replied Mackay.

"Correct."

"Like Affendi."

"Correct."

"Bastard."

"Correct."

"Shall I stand the lads down then Sarge?"

"Might as well, those sods won't be back, that's for sure" sighed an obviously disappointed Baron. "Just leave one on guard in case."

"I'll get rid of that bloody aerial, too. Dam thing's bugger all use anyway."

"Yeah, we'll start striking camp now too; we'll be away shortly in any case. And tell Moran I'm not having those bloody snake skins stinking the grot out back at Sundar as well. He can leave the buggers here." Exactly on time Baron and the platoon edged their way from the swamps into the main river and joined up with their waiting colleagues,

"Anyone see any action then?" Baron yelled across to the nearest boat.

"Not a whisper" came the reply.

"Reckon we got the nearest to making contact then lads" the jovial Sergeant beamed.

"Stuff the action" said Lewis.

" Just get me an' Scouse back to Sundar in one piece."

"Don't worry my ansomes, the war's over for you two now. Reckon you'll be off to Brunei tomorrow or the day after, you'll see."

"Bloody hope so."

"Won't you miss all this beautiful scenery, the trees, rivers, flowers and us?" asked Mackay."

"Like a hole in the head."

"Don't you mean will we miss the mossies, leeches, sweat, snakes, lack of food and water and the stench of Ginge's feet?" added Lewis.

"Here, my feet don't stink" protested Luther.

"Not many, Benny; they bloody hustle."

"Crap."

"Yeah, that too. it'll be nice to have a decent bugger without some weirdie and a squadron of bleedin' flies descending on it."

"What exactly will you miss then?" asked Baron.

"Fuck all, is the short answer. Well, I suppose the memory of you buggers will linger for a while; but not long, once we get down the Spotlight, ay, Scouse?"

"Not a chance; although we'll definitely miss a certain Mister Kipling and his rantings."

"At least we've learned how to play bloody Contract Bridge though, if fuck all else."

"Can't you drive this bloody thing faster Sarge" yelled Laker. "I'm bleedin' starving'"

"The stomach that walks speaks......" commented Luther.

"We'll nip out and check the stuff is OK while the others are sorting out their gear, Scouse."

"Right. Better leave it where it is for now though. Be a bit risky getting it into our packs again in daylight. Wait until nosh time then we'll slip round an d get it. You go and have a quick look see now. Take a spade, it'll look good if any bastard sees you and no sod is gonna come within a mile of you having a crap" laughed Lewis.

"Funny. OK then. Didn't think we'd be off tomorrow though did you?"

"Nah, but I'm not complaining, are you?"

"Me? Complain? Never happen."

"I just heard a buzz that the Company could be out here for another three months before being relieved. That'll please the bloody married fads no end."

"Serves them right for getting hitched in the first place. Stupid bastards. All the spare fanny there is in the world and they want to tie themselves to one piece for the rest of their natural. Ain't right."

"Maybe they're in love or something.

"Bloody must be. Can't imagine waking up every morning with the same bird lying beside me though, 'specially if she's got BO or bad breath all the time, and her bloody head in rollers. Stone me."

"Romantic bastard, ain't yuh."

"Well, look how long they take to get ready for a bleedin' run ashore. Fuckin' ages. All that paint gets slapped on and there's all the business with the curlers and tongs and things; enough to drive yuh bloody crackers. No. I like to see the fanny all tarted up and ready for action, not have to wait all bloody night for it."

"One day some bitch will trap you, you'll see."

"Balls. I'm going to share my beautiful body with all the tarts that want it, not just one."

"Time will tell" said Lewis. "Come on, let's go and sit by the river and watch the turds float by."

"Now who's a bloody romantic?"

"That's it then Scouse; all stowed away and ready for spending."

"And nobody any the wiser. We wuz bloody lucky too, ay?" Fancy building a bloody shithouse right next to where we buried it. Would've fucked us right up if they'd put it any nearer."

"Yeah, another two feet and they'd have dug the bugger up themselves and we'd have shit it. Literally."

"Hang fire, the lads are coming back. let's go and get our nosh now." That evening, from nowhere Baron produced a bottle of Bells whisky and a bottle of the local Brandy Wine. "Where the hell did that come from then Sarge?" asked Lewis.

"Keeping it for a special occasion, wasn't I? And getting rid of you two bastards tomorrow is a special occasion, right lads?" grinned Baron.

"Organisation, Sarge, ay?" said Laker.

"You're learning at last my son." beamed Baron. "Come on then, get stuck into it, then we can listen to the reminiscences of our two departing colleagues and all about how they're going to miss us all in Singers and UK."

"That'll be the fucking day. But we will drink a long lingering toast to you all in the Spotlight the first night we get down Nee Soon."

"Yeah" added Lee "And I'll definitely be thinking of you all when I have my first bag off."

"God help those poor bitches in the shacks when you get back." grinned Mackay.

"What's the betting you catch the boat up before you leave for Blighty?" laughed Laker.

"Yeah, probably get the black syph off No-Nose" added Moran.

"Nice shower of bastards, aren't you?"

"Yeah, thanks for the kind thoughts." An hour later when the alcohol had run out, Baron insisted that as it was their last night, they should have the honour of reading a poem each from Rudyard to the platoon, so amid great laughter at their mimicking of Baron, Lee and Lewis both pleasantly under the influence, ended their last evening in the company of their pals.

"This is it then my ansomes; the parting of the ways. Good luck to both of you. See you in dear old Guz" grinned Baron shaking hands with first Lee then Lewis. "And bloody behave yourselves in Singers before you piss off." he added.

"Yes dad."

"Cheeky sod."

"Believe it or not we'll miss you bastards, right Scouse?"

"That won't last long once you get down Nee Soon and are blowing your bloody brains out with No-Nose" chided Laker.

"No chance. It's big Mary for me" said Lee.

"Look after yourselves lads" said Lewis "and at least try and get bloody Affendi this time and not give him a weeks' notice that you're around." he laughed.

"We'll try, and don't forget all those little errands we gave you" said Baron. "Pop round and tell the missus and the kids that we're OK and soon be on the way back" he added.

"OK, no sweat. And thanks for the piss-up last night. Where the hell you got that lot from I don't know, but I don't expect you'll tell us, will you? No, I thought not. Well, so long lads, all the breast." The handshakes and good wishes over, Lee and Lewis clambered into the dugout which was to take them back to Brunei.

"Give big Mary one for me" yelled Laker.

"Don't forget to post the mail" called Linden.

"Send us a postcard from Guz" laughed Baron, and the craft pulled away and headed towards Brunei Bay and Headquarters, the cheering, waving gathering on the bank slipping from view as they rounded the bend.

"Well, we're on the way now Scouser"

"Thank fuck; but I'll miss the lads though. Still, we'll probably all meet up again in 41 in Bickleigh."

"No doubt."

"Can't wait to get into Singers though."

"Yeah, and get that dough changed for UK money too."

"I've been thinking about that. I reckon the best thing to do is stow it away until the last minute. Don't really want that kind of cash floating around too bloody long, do we?"

"No, but there's lots of things I wanna buy before we piss off, like Rabbits and things" said Lee.

"Don't let it burn a hole in your pocket, mate. We've got three months back pay to come yet, so we'll have stacks of cash to play about with."

"A few nights in the Spotlight will soon shift that lot" said Lee.

"If we run short we can always cash a bit, but I doubt that we'll need to. We'll only be in Singers a few days at most before we fuck off, surely."

"Never know with this bloody mob; probably get sent straight to bloody Aden or somewhere tomorrow" moaned Lee.

"That's one hole I don't want to see ever again. The sooner 45 pull out of there, the better; don't want my next commish there, that's for sure."

"Anyway, let's get this bastard over with first. So what are we going to do with the loot? Be a bit dodgy in the billet. Some bright bastard might just stumble across it or they might still have Rounds now and again."

"Reckon the best place would be the Store. No bugger goes there and there's only Smithy on rear party looking after it. We can soon draw him away from it while we stow the stuff in one of the machine gun boxes, then lock it with our own key, just in case he had a bleedin' brain storm and decides to clean a gun for a change."

"Fat chance. He must be the laziest berk I've ever known."

"Yeah, I reckon that's the best idea then. Mind you, do you think we can afford to lure him out with the price of a free goffer?" laughed Lewis.

"I think we can just about stoop to that, don't you; after all, one must speculate to accumulate, what?"

"Remember our last little speculation, in Devizes at that Pongo camp?"

"How could I forget? Bloody good effort that was. 'Organisation' as Baron would have put it."

"Yeah, those stupid pongos fell for that fire alarm routine dead easy, ay?" chuckled Lewis.

"Funny part was, the buggers actually helped us load up the waggon with all their booze and fags out of the NAAFI. I mean, how were they to know the driver was a civvy hired to do an ordinary job as a driver even though he was bent as arseoles and further, your brother?"

"That was the coolest few hundred quid I ever made" grinned Lee."

"Subtle, so subtle, my son. We'll have to pull that one again sometime, ay?"

"A mission carried out with all the military precision expected of Her Majesty's Royal Bloody Marines"

"Perzackerly." Now they were approaching the jetty from which their episode in Borneo had begun and it was with poignant memories that they silently recalled the events after they boarded the two LCVs from this same place.

"ere we are again......" Lewis let the words drift away.

"Only this time we're not shitting ourselves" added Lee.

Back to Singers

The jetty was heavily populated with military personnel of all persuasions; the Navy seemed to have complete dominance but were well protected by Army and even some RAF men.

"What's the bloody Brylcreem boys doing here then?"

"Probably on another fucking ban-yan like they are all over the bloody world, should have joined those bastards and had a cushy life, shouldn't we?" said Lee.

"At least they always eat."

"Where's all the bleedin' WAAFS then?"

"They'll be earning a fortune on Virgins Corner back in Singers no doubt." A Landrover had been sent to meet them and transport them over to the Headquarters at the school. On their arrival, they were allotted a billet in one of the classrooms that was acting as a transit base, and given a sleeping bag and mosquito net with their camp bed,

"Such luxury" joked Lewis. "Make a change to wake up not stinking in a filthy bag, ay?"

"Hello lads; how goes it?" asked one of the younger marines that had recently arrived from UK and was undergoing a jungle acclimatisation course of lectures with other new arrivals.

"You two were at Limbang weren't you? What was it really like?"

Lee's long hard stare made the young questioner uneasy.

"Suffice to say I hope you never have the same experience" he replied.

"Wasn't that bad was it? I heard you had a bloody ban-yan there."

Hardly had the words left the young marines mouth than Lewis had him by the throat, pushed up against the wall.

"You ever say that again and I'll wring your bloody neck. Little bastard, what the hell do you know?"

"Alright, don't get carried away" stammered the youth.

"I just heard that you all had a good time on the boats, what with them all loaded up with booze an' all." Releasing his grip, Lewis threw the marine aside.

"Leave him Lewy, he doesn't understand fuck all yet. But he will."
And turning to the youth

"Not an HW rating are you?"

"No, just a gash hand. I tried for a Heavy Weapons course but they wouldn't have me for some reason. Don't know why."

"Just as well. Do yourself a favour, and don't talk like that around S Company lads or you'll be sorry, understand?" Visibly shaking, the marine replied in the affirmative and sidled out of the billet.

"Come on Lewy, lets get over to Willie's grot and see if he's got any buzzes on our flight back to Singers." Patterson was found in his makeshift office wallowing through a mound of Drafting and Movements orders and countless signals arranging and cancelling air movements to and from Singapore. "Hiya lads, how goes it? Glad to be back in civilisation, if you can call this bloody madhouse anything like civilised?"

"Yeah. How're you going Willie? Any news on our flight yet?"

"Well, I'm trying like fuck to get you both on a Beverly that's going back at 0900 tomorrow, but some bloody Navy pig is insisting that his rotten little flunkey goes with him, which will leave only one seat free. There's one due out the next day though, so if you two lovers particularly want to go together I can stick you on that one, OK?"

"That'll do us, ay, Lewy?"

"Yeah, why not. One more day in this dump won't make a lot of difference will it?"

"Nah, and I'm sure a certain clerical arseole we know has got some booze stashed away somewhere, you know what I mean, pal?"

"Now I wonder just who you mean?" replied Lewis.

"OK you two bastards, come over to the grot tonight after nosh and maybe, just maybe, I might be able to produce the odd dram or two."

"Good lad Willie. See you later then. Ta la."

"See yuh."

"Lee, Lewis get over to the Intelligence Officer immediately."

"Very good Sergeant Major."

"Now what the fuck have we done?"

"Christ knows. Probably a bollicking as usual."

"But we haven't done anything this time, have we?"

"Not that I can remember. Come on, let's see what the buzz is."

The Intelligence 'office' was behind the same curtains on the stage of the school assembly hall that Lewis had previously heard the brutal interrogations taking place when he had brought the injured sailors to Brunei. Uneasily, they climbed up onto the stage and gently eased the curtains aside and looked around.

"Ah, come in you two" called the Intelligence Officer from the far corner of the stage.

"Sit down" he said pointing to two chairs that had been drawn up to the desk opposite him and the civilian sat next to him. Of medium height with jet black hair and most prominent thick square jaw below piercing pale blue eyes, Captain Lock then proceeded to introduce the civilian. "This is Mr Warner who is a journalist from the Sunday Mail, England."Lee and Lewis eyed the short squat man with the pince-nez and round ruddy complexion who was perspiring profusely at the side of the IO, and nodded a 'hello'.

"Mr Warner" continued the IO

"has been sent out to Borneo to get some inside stories on the action as it happens here, and as you two have been through three months of intensive active service in the jungle I have selected you to provide him with the information on your experiences. Obviously there are areas which will remain classified which is why the interview is taking place here and why I shall remain present throughout. Please continue, Mr Warner."

"Good afternoon gentlemen" pince-nez started.

"I hope you are both well and no doubt looking forward to your repatriation to the United Kingdom" he grinned, his beady eyes darting from one to the other of the marines.

"Now, what I am after in particular is more in the being of human interest stories, Captain Lock has told me that you two were involved in the landings at Limbang and that is the sort of area I'm interested in. What I'd like to know is what was it like, your own personal feelings as young men thrown into action; the tension, your fears, if any" he quickly added "and generally what sort of things went through your minds at that time, especially seeing your friends so tragically killed and the enemy also. Make it nice and interesting and as juicy and gory as you like, OK?" he grinned.

This time it was Lee who snapped into action a fraction before Lewis

"You little bastard" he shouted at pince-nez.

"Juicy, gory? You arseole." leaning right over the desk, his face an inch from the startled reporter he bellowed

"I'll tell you what it was fucking like, fucking awful. Not interesting, or juicy or gory, but plain bloody awful, bastard."

"Marine Lee" started the IO. In vain.

"You're getting shot at by these rebels and all the time you're crapping yourself, Yeah, some blokes actually shit themselves in fear, You shoot anything that moves and it dies right there in front of you. And you don't give a toss who or what it is either. Men, women, kids, dogs anything; because it just might be the enemy with you in his sights, so you kill it to make sure, Not just one bullet but as many as you loose off in one go. Later, when you get hardened to it you kill more thoroughly and coldly. Now, a whole belt or magazine gets pumped into the victim, just to make sure, And you make sure, No room for the slightest doubt, No time. Just kill the bastards before they kill you. And still blokes get killed, Booby traps, mines and any other method these bastards can use, And what the fuck is round the next bend? What's in the jungle just ahead of you? Who's got you in their sights from that block of flats? Are you running out of ammo? Pray like fuck that you don't get a stoppage on the gun. Yeah, and you still shit yourself at the slightest strange sound. But now you're ruthless to a degree you didn't imagine possible. You hate. For the first time in your life you really hate. No time for sleep. Food? What the hell is that? Smash a store open and find some liquor, It helps, but you daren't have too much. Makes you tired. And careless, Can't afford to be careless; and live. Then there's a moment's relaxation. But you don't. Too scared and wound up. Sleep? Sometimes it comes, but it don't last long. Dreams, fighting. All the time, every night someone wakes up screaming and sweating and is held down and cooled down by his mates. Can't find your weapon in the dark when you wake up in a sweat. Must kill the bastards, quick! Then there's the swamps, leeches, snakes and the bastard mossies that don't give you a minute's peace. Doze and you start dreaming again; the bodies riddled with bullets, some almost cut in half by the bullets from what can only be a machine gun, so you know it was you that killed them." Easing away from the reporter, Lee finished

"Juicy enough for you? Nice and interesting? You fucking morons;

get the hell away from me before I stick my rifle up your nice and interesting arseoles."

"Get him out of here, Lewis" ordered a subdued Lock.

"OK Scouse, let's go. Over now" guiding the still shaking Lee away from the desk.

"Bastards."

"Some of you have, I know" said Captain Lock to the departing group of marines

"been through a very traumatic time. But it is your duty as Royal Marines and men, to learn from these experiences and so improve your worthiness to yourselves, your Corps and your country. Now in conclusion may I thank you all for your efforts, and on behalf of the Commanding Officer wish you a safe return to Singapore and the United Kingdom. Dismiss them RSM please."

"See yuh, lads. All the best."

"Cheers Willie. Save you a pint of Scrumpy in the London Bar."

"Piss off."

The giant Beverly lumbered along the runway, shuddering as the huge underbelly finally raised itself off the tarmac and headed up above the ensuing jungle, into the low clouds and out of sight.

"Goodbye fucking Borneo."

"Good riddance, too."

"Wasn't so bad really Scouse, Apart from that first lot at Limbang, Won't forget that in a hurry. That's for sure, Had some good laughs along the way though, didn't we? Remember Baron crunching the boat? I nearly pissed myself at that."

"Yeah. Good old Baron. Hope he gets drafted back to the same unit as us, if he ever leaves the Far Flung, that is, making so much cash, they' ll have to drag him and the kids out."

"Pity we can't all stay teamed up for all our service like the pongos."

"Dunno, I reckon we'd really get on each other's tits after a while."

"Which brings me to our favourite subject. Women for the use of. What's the programme tonight, or need I ask?"

"Usual I reckon; shit, shave, shower and shampoo and ashore."

"First stop the Spotlight?"

"Naatch."

"Then on to the delights of Boogie Street?"

"I reckon there must be a fair chance , what you say?"

"Agreed."

"Time for a smally kip?" Agreed.

"Oh God. And life was so peaceful here."

"Hiya Smithy. How's things?"

"They were Ok, Now I'm not so sure."

"Miserable old sod. That's a fine way to greet the conquering heroes after they've just won the war."

"You two couldn't fight your way out of a paper bag, Anyway, what was it like over there? Heard some pretty grim stories back here."

"I can think of some better ways to spend a holiday. Wasn't too bad in the end though."

"When are your flights then?" the stout, greying Marine enquired.

"A week to wait or there about. So the bastards didn't waste any time in getting us on the bloody guard roster. One in three ain't it?"

"About that. Bloody grim. Sooner be over there with you lot."

"Don't you believe it. You don't realise how good it is to see a bloody shower after three months and to actually smell real food being butchered by those excuses for chefs."

"We've got two rest days before we do any duties, so I reckon we'll only catch up a couple at the most."

"That's if the bloody flights are on time. How've they been?" added Lee.

"Not too bad, they're flying a load of pongos out from Germany and the UK so there's plenty of empties going back. You should be pretty well on time, I guess."

"Thank Christ for small mercies."

"I was just going up the NAAFI for stand-easy. Coming?"

"You go ahead. We'll just give our SMGs a quick wipe over and a pull through and join you in a minute. We'll lockup, don't worry."

"OK. Don't nick fuck all though, will you?"

"Who us?" Lee and Lewis replied in unison. "How could you think such a thing?"

"Easy. Dead easy."

"That should do Ok Lewy, Safe as houses, Soon as we get an exact flight date we'll whip it into a bank in town and cash in."

"Right. Now let's piss off before Smithy comes wandering back."

Joy and Despair

"Have you missed me then Mary?"

"Me miss you velly much Scouse saab. No-One else good jig-jig like Scouse saab. No one look after Mary like you. Mary love you."

"She's probably said that to every hairy arsed matelot and pongo that's crawled through her in the last three months" laughed Lewis.

"Nah, you've stayed true to me haven't you darlin'?" prompted Lee bouncing the delicious young Chinese girl on his knee, one hand stroking the vast expanse of bare thigh exposed by the slit in the girls' cheong-san while the other cupped her breast.

"Me love you, no-one else super Scouse"

"Stone me, She's been on the bloody opium again."

"Nah, it's pure lust. And who can blame her?" laughed Lee.

"But I'm afraid you'll have to wait a while for my favours, beautiful. Me and Lewy saab must go to the city first on velly important business. Won't be long."

"You no go to other girl, ay?" pouted the girl.

"Of course not, How could I? Back velly soon" mimicked Lee rising from the seat at the bar and running his hands all over the girl's body as he kissed her passionately. Forcing her hands from behind his neck he and Lewis headed for the door, promising to return as soon as their business was completed, and made their way out towards the road where they hailed a 'fast black' taxi.

"Quiet in there. eh?" commented Lewis,

"Yeah, none of the lads around, that's why."

"C'mon, lets get down the Brit Club. Must be loads of white trash around on their own, what with all the units being over in Borneo. Bound to pick up something, ay?"

"Yeah, VD probably." Soon they were seated on the first floor balcony of the Britannia Club in the heart of downtown Singapore nonchalantly casting their eyes over the unusually large number of white women in the bar.

"Plenty around, Lewy"

"Most of it is a bit rough though, ain't it?"

"Getting bloody fussy in yer old age ain't yuh? A few more Tigers and you'll crawl through anything."

"You're fuckin' safe, that's for sure" his companion laughed.

"How about these two then?" said Lee as two younger women approached,

"Hello darlin'. Wanna join us for a bevy or several?"

"Awa an' piss up ma kilt laddie" the shorter of the two replied.

"Charming. Bleedin' charming. Lovely girl. Come home and meet mummy."

"Caber tossing, kilt swinging, porridge yaffling, haggis waffling cow. I wouldn't piss up your kilt if you were the last whore in Boogie Street" Lee shouted after the women.

"Slags."

"Hey, did I hear yuhs screeching at a Scots lassie fella?" a voice said at Lee's shoulder the owner of which was a very small, very drunk and a very patriotic member of the Queens Own Scottish Borderers.

"Piss off Jock."

"I'm a Scots laddie from Fife an' aal nae hear a soon agin a lassie frae ma hame" he burbled swaying to such an extent that only the back of Lee's chair appeared to keep him upright.

"Just sling yer hook sunshine and do us all a favour, eh?" said Lewis.

"We've just come for a quiet run ashore, so leave us alone, there's a good laddie."

"Ah'll tak the pair of yees ootside just the noo, teach ya a lesson ye'll no forget in a wee while and no mistaken."

"This prick is getting right up my throat," Scouse.

"Me too." As they were both aware, beneath them on the ground floor was the swimming pool, situated below the balcony on which they were now seated. Instinctively nodding agreement and with little hesitation, each grabbed a shoulder and arm of their antagonist, ran him to the balcony and threw him over, The shrieks of the females present soon subsided as the unfortunate Scot made a resounding splash in the water, narrowly missing the side of the pool en route.

"Time we left, I think" said Lewis.

"Agreed. Let's go." While everyone in the bar peered over the balcony at the Scot being unceremoniously hauled out of the water by a waiter, Lee and Lewis headed down to the main entrance and across the road into the famous Raffles Hotel.

"Don't really fancy a punch up right now, do you?" said Lewis, smiling.

"Nah, just big eats and a piss up and a bint from the Boogie will do me" Lee agreed.

"I bet that little bastard shit himself in mid air, eh?" laughed Lewis. "Scots arseole. Why are little bastards always so aggressive, especially Scots buggers."

"Their size makes them feel inferior I reckon, Scotsmen give me the shits at the best of times, anyway. It's the Welsh buggers I can't handle, That bloody accent must be the worst in the world. Bloody awful."

"They're nearly always stroppy as well" agreed Lee.

"Yeah. Plenty of fanny in here tonight, eh?" Lewis changed to his favourite subject as they crossed the plush carpet floor to the bar area. "I could do one or two of these a favour and no mistake, though it's all pigs trash." Making short work of two Tigers, they eyed the females sat at the ornately carved tables between which several smartly clad waiters in their immaculate whites glided with trays of drinks.

"Fuck it" Lee suddenly exclaimed

"Let's try the bold approach" and to his companion's amazement he crossed to a table Lewis had not seen from his angle, between some decorative palms situated in the far corner of the room, and at which two very attractive women were seated. Catching up with Lee as he reached the table, Lewis heard his pal's opening remark of

"Now how would you two gorgeous young ladies like to spend a night on the town with two battle weary young commandos who have just returned from the Front?" Cringing, Lewis waited for an instant dismissal, but was pleasantly surprised to hear the taller of the two remark, having studiously scrutinised the marines

"Why not?" Turning to her blonde companion she added

"One might find it an amusing interlude, what?"

"One must admit a certain intrigue at so bold an approach, and one

207

is rather bored at this moment in time with one's spouse elsewhere" the other replied.

"Well, this one and that one" said Lee nodding to the smiling Lewis "are about to take Singapore apart and would feel highly honoured if both you 'ones' would care to join us. How about it gal?"

"Rough , but not unattractive" the blonde said. And turning to her friend

"Should one?"

"Perhaps. In such rugged company, one should be reasonably safe. Would you care to join us for a drink and we will assess the situation?"

"Delighted, Duchess. Move over then" said Lee squeezing alongside the tall, dark woman seated on one side of a cubicle seat while Lewis edged the blonde into a corner as he sat beside her and opposite the others.

"Good here, ain't it?" said Lee.

"What's your poison then? Looks like a drop of the hard stuff to me, right?" he added inspecting her glass.

"Waiter, top 'em up there's a good lad and two more Tigers."

"So what's your names then?" ventured Lewis.

"My name is Judith and my friend Sabine" said the blonde in reply. "And yours?" she arched her delicately pencilled eyebrows at Lewis.

"I'm Lewy and that's Scouse. We don't have other names. Different ain't it?" he laughed.

"Where the hell did you get a name like Sabine, anyway Duchess?" responded Lee.

"Subtle ain't he?" stated Lewis laughing.

"My father was a Russian and my mother Polish. They concocted it between them, I imagine." her rather thinnish yet strikingly good looking face breaking into a most attractive smile which immediately increased Lee's heart rate.

"Well." said Lewis addressing Judith

"What were your plans tonight then before you were captivated by our stunning good looks, dazzling conversation, humour, wit and charm?"

"We had no definite arrangement, just a quiet relaxing evening in these exquisite surroundings" she replied brushing a wisp of hair from her heart shaped face, to which Lewis was becoming addicted by the moment.

"Well, we were going off to Boogie Strasse for a bit of a rave up" chipped in Lee.

"Fancy it, or maybe somewhere else?"

"Is there anywhere else in Singapore?" laughed Lewis.

"You'll appreciate that spending so much time in the jungle and on active service fighting for our Queen and Country that we don't often get the time to socialise a great deal" Lee grinned.

"Boogie Street doesn't really come to life until after midnight, so why don't we all repare to Orchard Road and visit the Orchard Pub. It is rather charming and so English" said Sabine.

"And awfully romantic" added Judith casting a side glance at Lewis.

"Well, I'm all for a bit of romance" said Lee.

"All in Favour?"

"Yah, one hasn't been there for a while" answered Sabine.

"OK then one, let's go." Outside the hotel there was no sign of disturbance across the road at the Britannia Club so, all spilling into a taxi, they set off.

The Orchard Hotel was one of the better hotels in Singapore although by no means as elegant as the Raffles. Set in a backdrop of fringed palms with coloured lights dancing in the cool, welcome, breeze the pub part of the hotel was usually very busy by this time of the evening,. But with so many troops away from Singapore, tonight it was much quieter and with none of the normal difficulty, they obtained a booth and ordered their drinks.

"We're not likely to bump into any of your officer type friends are we?" said Lee

"As one feels at this precise moment in time, one doesn't give a toss" Sabine replied to their surprise.

"Now you're talking my kind of language, Duchess" said Lee slipping his arm around her shoulders.

"If you don't mind me asking" said Lewis to Judith

"where exactly are your men at the moment?"

"Both have been in Borneo for a month. They are Royal Engineers.

Captains, actually."

"And we miss them terribly" added Sabine.

"You could've fooled me" laughed Lewis.

"Making hay while the sun shines?"

"One must carry on living, after all. Can't shut oneself off from society and live in total seclusion, what?"

"Couldn't agree more; got to keep in fine fettle for when the conquering heroes get home, eh?"

"Precisely. Another drink, perhaps?"

"My pleasure."

A pleasant evening ensued as the foursome got to know each other. This was, however concluded at Lee's pronouncement that the pangs of hunger had become unbearable and that he must eat something soon or die of malnutrition. So, without further ado they hired a fast black and headed for Boogie Street.

Boogie Street. A veritable cacophony of colour, noise and pulsing, throbbing vitality never still, never at peace from early dawn to the next. Bars and cafés spilled onto the pavement as each shopkeeper filled his allotted space to the full with chairs and tables which, as usual were filled to capacity with all manner of servicemen and woman in various states of sobriety, some eating the delicate and colourful dishes that were to be had, others merely consuming glass upon glass of Tiger beer. A pulsating mass of Malays, Chinese and Europeans and scatterings of other races comprised the thronging mass while over the banter of the many languages records blared from radios and juke boxes all along the street.

After luckily grabbing a table just as others rose to leave it, the four settled down to wait for service while watching the constantly changing scenes around them, not in the least the 'Kyeties', transvestites who paraded up and down the street in the most stunning dresses and costumes and who many an unsuspecting sailor or soldier had waltzed away only to realise his mistake after paying his irretrievable 'fee'.

Lee immediately ordered his favourite Nasi goreng while Lewis and the women settled for the more traditional Sweet and Sour and soon they were surrounded by an array of the most fascinating variety of side-dishes encompassing the whole table.

"God, we'll never manage this lot" exclaimed Sabine.

"Watch my tracer" replied Lee scooping great mounds of rice into his mouth, followed by great gulps of Tiger.

Constantly they were harried into playing Noughts and Crosses by one of the constant flow of children that tugged at their sleeves. and each time they ventured a game, they lost to the little experts at a fee of twenty cents.

"These little sods make a bloody fortune down here" said Lewis.

"Not as much as the Kyeties, that's for sure. Some of them are quite beautiful" observed Judith.

"Not going bent on us are you?" asked Lewis.

"Hardly. Beside, one never knows what one might catch, what?" For a further two hours they sampled the local delights, steadily consuming a variety of drinks on Lee's recommendation that one at least should prove to be an aphrodisiac, which in the case of Lewis and Judith seemed barely necessary as they constantly embraced, her now sat on his lap.

Lee and Sabine too, stole an occasional kiss and embrace so it was not unexpected that Lewis should ask

"Where are we going to spend what's left of the night then?"

"Have to be an hotel I reckon" volunteered Lee.

"I just don't care" said Judith

"just get there in a hurry while I'm in this frame of mind."

"No, we'll go to my place" said Sabine.

"The servants are away for the evening, but you must be gone very early before they return" she added."

"Suits me Sergeant Major. Right Scouse?"

"Settled. C'mon, let's go."

"So this is how the other half lives. Alright for some."

"Beats the hell out of the mess deck on bloody Bulwark, that's for sure" Lee agreed.

"Drinks everybody?"

"Thanks awfully old bean" mimicked Lewis.

"Why not let's celebrate our wonderful evening out and your safe return from the war zone in style? Champagne I think."

"Now this is what I call living" said Lewis.

"Actually, I think we'll take ours to the boudoir my dear, what?" Escorting Judith through the nearest door, Lewis returned seconds later with

"Trust me to pick the bloody kitchen! Night all."

"Pleasant dreams" called Sabine after them.

"Another glass darling?"

"No. All I want right now is you. Let's go."

"OK you two. Get up and get mobile. Report to the Movements Office in ten minutes. You're leaving at 2100 tonight. Move it."

"Really Sarge?" asked Lewis of the Duty SNCO.

"Really, now move your arses and get cracking" he ordered marching out of the room."

"What time is it Lewy?"

"Twelve thirty. Christ."

"Fuckin' hell. We've got to get a move on. The bloody banks shut at three and we've got to sort the dough out."

"No need to panic" Lewis assured his partner.

"First we'll get over to Movements and sort them out, then down the store and collect the money. We can return to our gear afterwards. A quick shower first, before we become the most eligible young millionaires in Jannnerland, what?"

"Talking of which, fucking good night last night, eh?"

"Yeah. Better give them a ring and cancel our date for tonight before we fuck off. Pity, they was a couple of right tasty birds those two."

"Still, plenty more where they came from. Roll on Blighty."

"Go and get the goffers then Smithy. I'll pay" said Lee.

"Getting bloody generous in your old age aren't you?"

"Call it a going away present."

"Back in a minute. Don't nick fuck all."

"Is it all there, Lewy?"

"Now when did Smithy ever bother to take a gun out and clean it when there was no fucker around to watch him? Course it's all here."

"Good. I'll take it up to the Guard room and order a fast black while you wait for him. Should be in Singers by three easy."

"Which bank shall we take it to then? They all look the bloody same to me" said Lee staring at the numerous banking houses that confronted them in the centre of the business section of the city."

"The nearest bugger I reckon. Come on." said Lewis starting into the tall imposing building directly opposite them, which, with its huge pillars and marble floors lent Lewis to remark that it was more like a palace than a bank, Crossing to a window behind which sat a sleight, bespectacled Malay, Lewis, clutching the polythene bag containing the money close to his chest, joined the small queue waiting to be served.

"Taking his bloody time, ain't he?" moaned Lee.

"Patience, my son. In a few seconds we'll be rich."

"Good,, I'm dying for a bloody Tiger. Got a mouth like No-Nose's crutch piece on a Sunday morning.

"Charming! Ah! At last. Here we go then. Good afternoon. Now listen carefully John, In this bag is a great deal of money. When you've counted it all, we want you to open two accounts in our names and divide the amount equally into them, OK?" Nodding agreement the cashier called one of his assistants to collect and count the money while he took the names of Lee and Lewis and proceeded to fill in the appropriate forms and paper work, Having given their names, the two marines crossed to the long wooden seats situated opposite the counter and sat down.

"What time do we have to be at the guardroom?" asked Lee.

"Seven thirty, fully booted and spurred.

"Just time for a final few wets in the Spotlight then. Good, maybe I can slip big Mary a crippler as well."

"Don't you ever give up?" laughed Lewis.

"That's as long as that bloody teller doesn't take too long. What the hell's he up to now? Lot of fuss and bother going on behind the bar."

"It's called a counter, not bar. You've got bars on the brain."

"Yeah, gold buggers. Hang on, he's calling us over." As they reached the counter the teller said

"Please to step into office at far end of bank. Manager wishes to see you."

"Thank you."

"What's this then Lewy?"

"Dunno. Maybe he just wants to know where we got all this cash from, or something like that."

"What the fuck has that got to do with him? None of his bloody business."

"Perhaps it has to be cleared or, I don't bleedin' know. Let's just go and see what he wants and play it off the cuff." Crossing to the office indicated by the teller, the two were greeted by another frail, but very smartly attired Malay who politely ushered them into his lavishly decorated office and invited them to sit in two plush chairs in front of his desk.

"Bit like our front room, ain't it" joked Lee, casting an approving eye around the office. "Where's the bar then?

"Give it a rest, Scouse" and addressing the manager

"so what can we do for you then squire?"

"This money which you have brought to my bank; may one ask exactly where it comes from?" stated the Malay.

"It's not nicked, if that's what you think" Lee burst forth.

"One casts no aspersions on your integrity gentlemen, but it merely interests one as to its origin." he left the end of his sentence in mid air; but seeing no response was forth coming, he continued

"Most rare, in fact."

"What the bloody hell is he on about?" said Lee becoming impatient,

"Please, we don't have a lot of time; we're on a flight to the UK tonight, so can we just get this cash banked away then we can push off, OK?" countered Lewis.

"Very well then gentlemen. Then I must tell you both that I am unable to receive this money into my bank and further, unable to open accounts for you with it."

"What's up with our money? Ain't it good enough for your bank then? We'll take the bloody lot somewhere else then. C'mon Lewy. You can stick your bloody bank, there's plenty of others." As the pair rose to leave, the manager said

"Gentleman, I am afraid that you will receive the same reply from any other bank in Singapore, or in the world for that matter."

"What the fuck are you on about?" shouted Lee aggressively.

"Gentlemen" the manager slowly replied

"that money you have is totally worthless, I am afraid."

"What!" yelled Lee and Lewis simultaneously.

"You must be fucking joking" added Lewis.

"Please to sit down gentlemen and I will endeavour to explain" the manager, now rather cautious after the marines' outburst, replied.

"I reckon you'd better, and a bit smartish" said Lee.

"Now gentlemen, have you indeed studied this money?"

"What the bloody hell for ? It's money aint't it? And plenty of it."

"We did count it, but that's about all" Lewis said more calmly than Lee at that time was capable of being.

"Well, had you had more time to check it more thoroughly" the manager continued

"you would have undoubtedly have noticed that at the top of each note are the words 'The Japanese Government Promises to Pay the Bearer the Sum of' and the amount of the note."

"I don't give a shit who promises to pay as long as some bugger does" continued Lee.

"Hang fire Scouse, Go on please."

"To explain further. In 1943 when Japan invaded our island, an integral part of her plan to bring about the collapse of the Government was to inflate the market with money. This she did, in the expectation that the Singapore and Malay economies would be ruined, as indeed proved the case, or nearly. Were it not for the brave Allied Forces such as your good selves, I suspect....." he shrugged..

"OK, OK, save the history lessons, So what you're actually saying then, is that this money is not worth a lot, right?" asked Lewis.

"Not even the paper it is written on. I'm afraid." replied the manager."

"I don't believe it" sighed Lee.

Turning to his comrade, Lewis said

"and we've carted this fucking lot the length and breadth of bloody Borneo for the last three months, all for sweet piss all."

"I'm afraid that is the position, sir." the manager quietly intervened.

"Fuck my old sea boots" Lee sighed again.

"Bloody shave off. What I wasn't going to do with that little lot in

Blighty."

"All that bloody bother hiding it and carrying it everywhere for stuff all."

"As you say sir, for nothing I am afraid."

"Thanks anyway" said Lewis rising and shaking the hand of the manager.

"Yeah, cheers" added Lee "Give us a couple of the notes as a reminder of what might have been.

"With pleasure sir."Outside the bank, Lewis broke the silence, "What a fuck up."

"Yeah" Lee agreed, "Still, at least we had a dream for a while."

"Good while it lasted, I suppose."

"And we are off to the UK tonight, eh?"

"Yeah."

"Spotlight?"

"Spotlight!"

The End